Claire Brock has a degree in Music fro
and also studied at Drumtech, where sh
in 2002/3. She has many years teaching
schools. Her students have been members of the National Youth
Orchestra and National Youth Wind Orchestra and have gone on to
study at specialist music institutions like the Royal College of Music, The
Institute and BIMM amongst others.

Claire has worked as a specialist Percussion Examiner for the London
College of Music, where she also trained other examiners in drum kit
examining, and composed pieces for their Drum Kit syllabuses. As well
as doing a lot of studio work she has toured much of Europe and played
with the likes of Robyn and Ex-"Sneaker Pimp" Kelli Ali.

Claire is in the process of writing a worksheets package for drum
teachers as well as a number of tuition books. For more info and updates
see:
www.brocksterdrums.com

How To Teach Drums

Your complete guide to becoming a successful
drum teacher

by Claire Brock

For Jack.
You gave me the best possible start and showed me
what a great drum teacher does.
I hope I made you proud.

Contents

Foreword

When I first sat in my studio reading through the first few pages of this book, two things hit me, firstly there is no manual for being a great teacher and secondly, why hasn't it been done before?

Teaching is a minefield in any subject, some do it right and some do it wrong but it's entirely subjective and nearly always based on end results. When you set out to embark on a career as an educator, what makes you a great teacher? I guess firstly has to be the passion to impart knowledge in the first place. Where do you get the knowledge? Through experience and years of study and of course, mistakes. Where do you start? There is the big question and one that I always get asked, here is the right place

Claire and myself share quite a few things in common but I'd say the one that appears more than most in conversation is our passion for good education. I've been teaching Claire for sometime now and not only is she an awesome player and educator but a great communicator. There are many more facets required to teach drums, not all teachers have them, and Claire has them by the bucket load…

If you want to build a solid foundation for teaching and being a better musician, you've made the right choice.

Craig Blundell

June 2013

Introduction

The music industry has gone through some massive changes in the last twenty years. For us drummers there are now fewer well paid gigs to go round, and unless you're one of the extremely talented, lucky few, then the traditional model of musicians making a living from playing alone no longer applies.

I don't think it's all doom and gloom as some do though, in fact, I don't think it's doom and gloom at all. In my experience if you're prepared to think outside of the box, work hard and develop your all round musicianship skills then there's just as many opportunities for you to earn a living as a musician today as there always has been.

Diversification is the key, earning your living from a combination of musical activities. These include: gigging, teaching, recording, workshops, producing, sound engineering, composing, arranging, being a drum tech and more. It can be enjoyable to do a whole combination of varied things involving drumming. I also wonder whether diversifying means you're able to have a longer career and makes you more resistant financially. If one area dries up you've hopefully still got the other areas bringing in money.

Teaching is a very common way to earn money as a drummer. Most musicians I know have taught at some point in their career. The amount of time you choose to spend teaching can be anything from one evening a week up to 7 days a week. You can use it to add a little extra regular income or earn a full time living. It's important to regard drum teaching as more than just a way of making money though and try to do it to the best of your ability. It's only fair to your students and yourself.

You might be thinking of getting into teaching but not sure how to start. Perhaps you're wondering what to teach and how best to teach it or you're unsure if you've got the necessary skills. Drummers often fall into teaching and even if we make a conscious decision to get into it (as you are) we usually start knowing how to drum, but not how to teach. Classroom teachers learn not only their subject, but how to teach it too.In this book I'm not only going to explain "How to Teach Drums", but cover the complete range of things you'll need to get up and running as a drum teacher. As well as helping you to decide for yourself what you want to teach and how, we'll discuss where you can teach, how to advertise and get new students, building a website, making YouTube videos and much more.

Online teaching using Skype is really starting to grow so there's information about that throughout the book too, including a dedicated section about the practicalities, equipment needed and anything you need to consider that's different to standard, 'offline' teaching.

Teaching can be both fun and rewarding and can actually help you improve as a drummer. By the end of this book you should have all the information you need to go out there and start earning some money.

What to Teach

There are three main areas I want to talk about as far as actual teaching goes. What to teach and how to teach it, which I've broken into two sections, general teaching ideas and specific drum based teaching.

For many drummers looking to get into teaching, what to teach can be one of the biggest questions. I've seen the question asked a lot on various drummer forums. There's no right answer to this, but I personally think there are some wrong ones! Here I'll give you a number of different ideas to help you, but my ultimate intention is to enable you to decide for yourself what you want to teach.

Firstly, if you've had any drum lessons yourself then look back at those, this might well help you start planning your lessons. What and how were you taught? What worked well and has really helped you, and which areas do you think perhaps you weren't helped enough with? Both the good and bad from your own experience of being a pupil will help you. If you haven't had drum lessons then think about any areas you initially struggled with and what would have really helped you when starting out.

There'll be certain students who come to you (often adults) who want to learn something specific ("I want to play *Back in Black*", "I want to read music" or "I want to be able to play more fills") in which case gear your teaching towards that. But for the most part your students will be beginners or people who already play drums but want to improve their all-round playing. In which case you need to make your own curriculum.

Don't be scared by this, it can actually be a fun process to work out what you want to teach and the order to teach it in. I'd call it your "*Drumming Timeline*". The majority of your teaching will be based around this, so spend some time on it.
Start by getting a few pieces of paper or opening a word doc, then write

down all the different things you can think of that drummers need to learn (be it beginners, intermediate or more advanced students). It can be technical stuff, types of beats, different styles, important songs, important drummers, co-ordination, timing, reading - just write down anything and everything that comes into your head. Keep coming back to it over a day or two and you'll end up with hundreds of things. Then try to put your list of all these different drumming concepts into a Timeline in the order that things need to be learnt.

I'll start you off with the first one: How to hold their drumsticks (or it could be the names of the drums, you'll have to decide for yourself!).

There's no point trying to teach someone *When the Levee Breaks* before they've learnt to play a basic rock beat. Likewise, students can't play *Cold Sweat* before they've learnt to open the hi-hats during beats. Again, take a bit of time to do this and don't worry, you can always swap stuff around. Once you start teaching you'll find there'll be things you need to add or that need to be in a different order, but that's fine, you've got yourself somewhere to start. This *Drumming Timeline* (what you want to teach and the order you want to teach it in) will form the basis of most of your teaching.

This is an example of how I might take someone from an absolute beginner towards intermediate level (we're going to add some specific songs later):

How to hold the sticks
Single Strokes
Double strokes
Names of each drum/cymbal
Reading 1/4 notes and rests
Basic bass drum technique
Reading 8th notes
Basic "8-beat" Rock beat
Reading 16th notes
Adding extra 8th note bass drums to a basic beat
Reading basic tom notation
Adding the crash cymbal to the beginning of beats (in preparation for adding it after fills)
Basic fills (some from written music but mainly focusing on making up simple one bar fills round the toms)

Paradiddles
Reading rhythms combining 8th and 16th notes
Left foot hi-hat (simple co-ordination exercises like LH LF together/ RH
RF together and adding alternate R/L feet under singles and doubles)
Half bar or shorter fills
Flams
Basic latin beat
Basic 16 beats
Open hi-hats in basic beats
Adding flams to fills
Adding extra snare 16th notes to beats to make simple funk beats
Basic 12/8 Blues beats
Turning paradiddles into beats
Adding extra bass drum 16th notes to beats

Obviously, things like singles, doubles, paradiddles etc will develop over time. Start off on the snare drum, then patterns round the toms (based on your ideas and then the pupils) and as time goes on you can speed them up, integrate them into fills etc. This way you'll constantly be improving a student's technique, speed, facility round the kit and creativity. Which brings us nicely to.....

Rudiments

The Percussive Arts Society website (www.pas.org) has a list of 40 drum rudiments. While some of these you probably won't find yourself teaching that often, there are a core that you'll be using all the time.

First and foremost, don't make rudiments boring! Explain that they're the foundations of drumming and integral to what we do, not just a combination of rights and lefts for students to play on the snare drum at the beginning of lessons then forget about (like a lot of pupils feel about scales on other instruments!). They can be a real aid to creativity if used in the correct way. It's the application of rudiments that makes them useful, interesting and fun. Drummers can practise them from the day they pick up sticks until the day they die and still have new things to work on and improve. Rudiments are great for almost everything. Technique, touch, co-ordination, grooves, fills, soloing, you name it.

Use a metronome and set certain targets for speed as students improve.

If you make sure students have the right technique and mechanics to play rudiments at a slow speed, it will make their life so much easier as they progress.

The main way to make rudiments interesting for students is to make them relevant. Yes, initially you'll teach them on the snare, but once they're confident with them and as your students improve, show them how they can be used as mentioned above for fills, grooves and soloing and always revisit them as students improve. Doubles are a great example. As a beginner, students will know them as just RRLL played as normal wrist strokes. As they advance as a player you can get them to use bounce doubles (making sure your students have good grip from day one will make this easier). Once they're fluent with bounce doubles you can then integrate this technique into any rudiment that contains a double at any point (paradiddles, paraddidlediddles, double paradiddles etc) and this will enable your students to play rudiments at much faster speeds making them good for chops, beats and soloing.

Here are some examples of how different rudiments can be used by students of different levels:

Beginner - Paradiddle fills
Intermediate - Double paradiddle grooves
Advanced - Swiss army triplets in solos à la Tony Williams

Whichever level your students are at, encouraging them to play rudiments on a practice pad can be very helpful as they can really concentrate on the motions required (full strokes, down strokes, up strokes, tap etc) without the distraction of sound. Also if they carry around a pair of sticks and a practice pad with them then they can practise anywhere, anytime without annoying people!

Drum Songs

One other really important area to look at is drum parts from specific songs. There are certain beats from certain songs that good drummers should just know. They've become part of our vocabulary as drummers, "drumming standards" if you like. Learning these not only improves your students' general drumming and can give them inspiration to make up their own beats, but can also help them understand what sort of beats are representative of different styles and bands.

Write down all the songs that you think drummers at different levels should know. Here are a few classics to get you started:
Back in Black
When the Levee Breaks
Cold Sweat
Superstition
Amen Break
50 Ways to Leave your Lover

More recent songs possibly vying for a place on the list:
Smells like Teen Spirit
Californication
Hysteria

Don't just focus on Rock and Funk, include other styles too, then songs like *Sing, Sing, Sing* enter the equation. Obviously it's subjective so everyone will have slightly different ideas about what counts as a 'must know' drumming standard. Once you've compiled a decent sized list it's time to go back and integrate them into your *Drumming Timeline* (you might already have some of these on there). Insert each song in the appropriate place, bearing in mind the different techniques and concepts students might need to have learnt before attempting a particular song. Alternatively, you could use some of these songs as a tool to introduce specific new ideas and techniques.

Beginners

On a couple of specific, special occasions, I have started teaching pupils younger than 7 years old. As a general rule though I don't start teaching children before that age as they're generally not big enough to sit at the kit and don't always have a long enough attention span (it's fun making noise on a kit and they can easily get distracted). Teaching beginners at the age of, say, 8 though I find is quite different than starting a 15 year old. It's worth taking the pace a bit slower for these younger students. I tend to do more general work on aural, pulse and musicianship in the early lessons to develop their all-round musical and drumming skills.

Here are a few suggestions for things to do with beginners. You'll probably spend more time on these with younger students, but some things are appropriate whatever the age.

Playing and copying. First of all on just one drum, then using a mixture of whichever drums and cymbals you wish. As well as you playing things for your students to copy, spend just as much time getting them to make things up for you to copy too. It means they're being creative from day one, gets them comfortable moving round the kit and will help their sense of pulse too. Don't forget to include playing at different dynamic levels. It can be a great way of introducing this idea and pupils usually manage to work out for themselves how to play quietly (even if they'd much rather be making a noise!). I also add diminuendos and crescendos too after a while as this will really help with their control. I usually start off doing just simple one bar patterns but there's no reason you couldn't do longer, more complicated patterns and use this idea with other non-beginner students too.

Playing single and double strokes along to music. This can be to mp3 backing tracks, their favourite songs, or playing something yourself on a guitar or piano, but getting them to play these basic rudiments at a slowish speed along with music will not only make the rudiments more interesting but it will get pupils used to listening to music and playing at a steady, given tempo.

"Jamming" or "Free-styling" (as some of my students like to call it). This can work better with some students than others, but is worth a go for younger students, particularly boys for some reason. You split up the kit so they have half and you have half (not actually moving drums, you just decide which ones each of you are allowed to play!). I tend to start with a repetitive rhythm and then let them jam along playing absolutely anything they like. If they get into a groove I'll change mine to complement it and so on; there's no rules as it's freestyling, but it can be a fun way of playing.

Adults

Depending on where you teach you might find yourself teaching very few adults or lots of adults. As far as your *Drumming Timeline* goes, this is the same whether you're teaching youngsters or adults. Teaching adult beginners can be really enjoyable and rewarding as often it's something they've wanted to do for years and have finally started doing. I sometimes find adults can be a little harder on themselves when struggling with things than children and teenagers. They're not used to learning new things and starting from scratch, so make sure you point out how they're improving, what they can now do that they couldn't a few weeks ago, and to be patient. Don't however be patronising, they'll see straight through it, so just be natural. Find out what sort of bands they're into and get them playing along to those songs as soon as possible to help their sense of achievement.

Bear in mind that adults who come to you who can already play usually will have a specific reason for wanting to start lessons with you, and often have a clearer idea of what they want to achieve. Perhaps they want to work on particular technique problems they have, want to have a greater vocabulary of fills, or are having problems with their timing. Make sure you start addressing these issues straight away, but that doesn't mean you can't also bring in other elements appropriate to their level from your *Drumming Timeline* to help their all-round drumming.

I remember that the first adult I started teaching, having already taught many younger students, was when I was at University. He was twice my age and I was a little nervous at first, but it was really enjoyable and we laughed and joked a lot. Just remember as with all your students you know more than them about drumming and have plenty of stuff to show and teach them.

Advanced Teaching

Teaching advanced students can be really enjoyable. You can work on some complex and challenging material and these students are often well motivated and practise a lot. Just make sure your own playing's of a high enough level or you'll soon be found out! Sometimes I've taught advanced students on a weekly basis, sometimes less frequently as they don't need their hand holding so much. This longer gap between lessons can give them more time to work on the concepts and ideas you're studying and assimilate them into their playing. Also I find lessons with these students tend to be longer, commonly an hour.

There are endless amounts of material you can work on and if you're an advanced player yourself then you'll probably have plenty of your own ideas. Polyrhythms, odd time signatures, linear playing and some really stretching co-ordination exercises can be good places to start. Styles like Prog and Fusion can be covered and there's so much great Latin stuff. Also make sure your students understand playing on, behind and in front of the beat.

Studying selected well-known drummers like Vinnie Colaiuta, Elvin Jones and David Garibaldi etc. can be worthwhile. Often, students at this level have favourite contemporary drummers like Teddy Campbell and Tony Royster Jr. whose drumming you can analyse and work on. The amount of YouTube videos of these guys playing really helps you to study what's individual about their style and breakdown some of their licks.

Here are a few books that you can work on with advanced students (there are hundreds more and also some great DVD's):

Tommy Igoe *Groove Essentials* (both books 1.0 and 2.0 - you can start using them from an intermediate level)
Gary Chaffee *Time Functioning Patterns* (this book includes *Fat Backs* - a must for any advanced drummer)
Gary Chester *The New Breed* (good for creativity)
Dave Weckl *Contemporary Drummer + One*
Marco Minnemann *Ultimate Playalong Drum Trax* (crazy time signature stuff with backing tracks)
Zoro *The Commandments of R&B drumming*
John Riley *The Art of Bop Drumming*

I've also recently been introduced to James Hester's *Mind Over Meter.* I haven't had much chance to work on it myself yet, but it definitely looks promising and a bit different.

Playing to Music

I've briefly mentioned getting your students playing along to music in a couple of other places, but I just wanted to stress how important it is. For the most part, drums aren't really a solo instrument, they're an ensemble instrument. It's a must for students to play along to songs, backing tracks and click tracks as often as possible. Being able to listen, keep a steady pulse, groove and lock in with the band are vital. By making playing along with music second nature to students, you're not only helping to develop these skills but also getting the opportunity to put various beats and fills you've been working on in lessons into a musical context. For example, if your student's been practising adding ghost notes in funk beats, then tie this in by playing these beats along to some funk tracks.

As well as using a mixture of songs chosen by both you and your students to play along to, if you play another instrument like guitar, bass or keyboard, then you could play this for your students to jam with. This way as well as getting used to playing to clicks, backing tracks and other recorded music, they're getting used to interacting with other musicians in a live environment and the additional skills they need for this.

Encourage students to play to music at home too. It can be a mixture of their favourite bands as well as just putting on the radio and playing to whatever comes on next. Now you can stream live radio on the internet, there's no shortage of possible tunes in all different styles for them to jam to. In lessons it's also quite fun to put your mp3 player onto shuffle and get students to play along to whatever song comes on next (this can be made even more entertaining if you've got any audio books on there - up pops a few lines of a Harry Potter book!).

One quick warning, just be careful you're not trying to get an 8 year old to play along to a song with a load of offensive language in it - not at all clever. Make sure the lyrics are appropriate for the students' age. Having said that though, I once had a 9 year old tell me one of his favourite tracks to play to at home was The Prodigy's *Smack my Bitch Up*, what can you do!

Getting students to play to a click is getting ever more important too. Not only is there the obvious benefit of improving their timing and inner clock, but there are now so many musical situations both live and in the studio that require drummers to play to a click, that it's a skill they need to develop. I always encourage students to imagine the click is someone stood behind them playing a cowbell and they're jamming along with them, rather than it being an inhuman constant electronic noise that they're fighting against. I recently heard of a student who went to study with a teacher I know. Previously, this student had learnt with a highly regarded player and teacher and could do plenty of really impressive

11

drumming acrobatics and technical licks around the kit, but when this new teacher asked them to play to backing tracks, they just couldn't keep time. They'd never practised with a click and seldom played to music, just worked on blinding technique and co-ordination. Now don't get me wrong, there's a time and place for licks and tricks, and good technique and co-ordination is important to us all, but if you can't put all this into a musical context and perform one of a drummers main tasks, timekeeping, then you're of little use to any band. You'd hope an advanced student would work this out for themselves, but more importantly for me it reflects really badly on their teacher.

Reading

As I write this section about reading (and I'm referring to standard music notation, not TAB) I feel like I'm getting into some sort of drumming marmite territory (for those who aren't British, it's spread made from yeast extract that you have on toast; you love it or hate it!), or Mac vs Pc. Whatever I write here, there'll be some people who don't agree with me, but there you go. I love Liverpool FC and The Doors and hate piccolo snares and not everyone agrees with me on that either! It's up to you to make up your own mind based on your personal experience, but I feel very strongly about it.

When you learnt French (or any other foreign language for that matter) at school, did you learn to read it? Of course you did (and if you didn't, shame on your teacher). Yes, speaking French is likely to be the skill you use most, but it's also rather useful to be able to read menus, signs and maybe even write a few words. Also, if your teacher's not writing stuff down, how are you going to practise at home unless you have a perfect memory for every word they said in the lesson; unlikely! For me, learning and teaching drums is exactly the same.

Especially if you're starting beginner students, my advice is to get them reading from the start and they won't give it a second thought. Basic notation that you'll most commonly use is easy to read and it's so much harder for drummers who are reasonably proficient to have to go back and start at square one with reading. Of course there are amazing drummers who can't read a note and have never had to. However as a teacher I firmly believe that it's our job to arm our students with as many useful musical and drumming skills as possible. Especially as far as teaching beats is concerned, the visual aspect of reading can really help people see where the different bass and snares etc. should be placed in relation to the hi-hats and means they know what to practise when they get home.

I'd say a quarter of the playing work I do probably involves reading. I play in a swing band where all the tunes are charted as well as quite a lot of pit and theatre work where reading is essential. Do you really want to close these opportunities off to your students from day one? The point being, you have no idea where your students' musical journeys are going to take them. They don't necessarily have to be the best readers in the world, but they should at least be proficient. Yes, I know being in bands and playing rock gigs generally doesn't involve reading, but it's still a good skill to have. Also, many of my more advanced students take Music as a subject at High school and as part of this have to perform solo drum pieces where the sheet music for their pieces must be handed to the examiner. If they can't read, learning solo drum pieces relies totally on memory.

That's not to say everything you do in lessons has to be notated, far from it. Getting your student's attention away from the written notes and using their ears is really important, drumming's an aural skill. It's also really important that your beginner students can play various different beats from memory and can play a number of fills with these beats, not rely solely on reading them. It's no use if one of their mates says "Oh yeah, you play the drums, do you want to jam with us?" and the drummer says "Oh I'd love to, but I'll have to pop home and get my drum music first", loser! It's all about balance.

Whatever your opinion might be as a drummer, as a teacher I don't think you can underestimate the importance of reading as a teaching tool, regardless of whether you think it's useful or necessary as a drumming skill. It means you can write things down for your students and they'll know what to practise when they get home. As I mentioned earlier, the visual element of beats and the fact that written music is really just a grid (especially as far as rhythms are concerned) can be helpful. Also, being able to read music will help your students when they need to transcribe tunes for themselves. Whilst few of your students will go on to earn a living as drummers, if they do, anything that gives them an advantage over the competition is a bonus and the ability to read is one of those.

There's also the added benefit that if your students want to play another instrument at any time in the future, then the rhythm reading skills they've learnt on the drums will be transferable. The same applies if they want to get into playing Orchestral Percussion too. Lots of schools have Wind Bands and Concert Bands, and again, some reading ability is normally needed for drummers if they want to join these.

I Can't Read, Can I Still Teach?

I've thought a lot about this and whilst there are probably a few teachers out there who don't read, due to the importance of students learning to read, I think you really must have at the very least a basic understanding of drum notation to teach. If you're serious about being a drum teacher (and I'm guessing you are as you're reading this book!) you must. I'm not saying you need to be the best reader or an overly fluent sight reader (great if you are, this is definitely the ideal) but to use a previous analogy, would you go to a French teacher who couldn't read French? If you really don't read drum music and want to get into teaching then I'd strongly advise you to get a few lessons with a good teacher in order to learn to read. It'll be money very well spent and hey, you can always get a feel for how they teach things and try to use these ideas in your own teaching. If you feel you can read a bit, but it's rusty, then most drum magazines have a section where they've got some notated beats etc., so pick up one of these and get playing. Again, time well spent. You could buy the drum music book of one of your favourite bands, this way you can improve your reading whilst playing beats and songs you like.

Drum Tabs

Drum tabs can be a useful teaching aid, but I'd use them with care. I personally think they're more complicated to read than normal drum notation. While I can sight read drum music better than reading a newspaper, you have to study drum tab a bit closer to see exactly which 16th note things fall on. Having taken the sensible decision to teach your students to read, make that primarily standard notation. However, as I mention elsewhere, tabs can be useful. If a student's got a certain song they'd like to learn and either you don't know it overly well or you're pushed for time, finding the drum tab online can be helpful. I find **911tabs.com** pretty good as it's got a big database of tabs from different sites, plus ratings. Here's where the caution comes in. Whereas printed music has hopefully been proof-read and is mostly written by a professional, drum tabs are just done by your average drummer, so some are distinctly better than others. And don't even get me started on how people try to explain repeats etc., it often confuses me even if I know the song! I've never printed out a tab that I think's right note-for-note, but they give you a place to start. Listen to the song (on Spotify or YouTube) and follow the tab to see what's right and wrong. It can help you learn a song faster. Then you can either show the beats to your student, help them listen to the song and work the main beats out themselves (which is what I would mostly do) or give them the tab if you think it's mostly right. Good students will understand how tabs work if you take a couple of minutes to explain them. Just emphasise to them that they're only a guide and to always use their own ears and judgement.

How to Teach - General

Itt's worth thinking about teaching in itself and the way people teach others a new skill (regardless of instrument or discipline). Whether you realise it or not, the way you choose to convey the ideas and material you have to your students will define everything you do as a teacher. To a certain degree this will develop with experience and you might well try different ideas over time to see what works best for you. It can also differ from student to student depending on how they learn best. Don't be turned off by this concept, it's just some ideas to consider that might help you along the way whether you're teaching for the first time or have some experience but are looking to improve and grow your business.

Spoon-Feeding or Giving a Fork?

One big area to think about is, are you going to spoon feed everything to your students or enable them to learn to think for themselves (i.e. give them a fork!)? Again, this is up to you and certain students will need more spoon-feeding than others, but what are they going to do when they're at home and you're not there to help them? By helping your students learn ways to work things out for themselves, you're enabling them to be more independent, learn a skill that will help them for years and making them much more able drummers as a result. A friend of mine recently trained to be a driving instructor and as part of the training they learnt how to teach or "coaching" as they called it. They were talking about pointing students in the right direction and giving them tips to help work things out for themselves rather than spoon-feeding everything. In a drum teaching situation this could mean letting students choose a song they'd like to learn (check it's something achievable, if not, maybe suggest they choose another - Muse's *Stockholm Syndrome* after a few months might be too early!). Rather than you going home and either working out every beat or printing out the drum tab (which you'll of course check is right) and then just playing the beats to your student for them to copy, teach them how to work out the main beats for themselves. For example, listening for higher or lower sounds to decide whether it's bass or snare, or which tom in the fill. Then listening out for the cymbal pattern in the beat (ride/crash/hi-hats?), then fitting the bass, snare and cymbal together. There'll be plenty of times when you'll need to help your students a bit, and this approach can take a little longer, but by doing this you've taught them not just one song, but how to listen and work out songs for the rest of their lives. Hey, you could even show them how to chart the song at the same time too!

I also think it's important to make sure your students aren't afraid to make mistakes. Mistakes are how we all learn and get better (if they didn't make mistakes, they wouldn't need lessons). Be encouraging, saying what they got right as well as pointing out how they can improve certain bits. I always give my students something specific to focus on when asking them to play something again. Rather than "give it another go" say for example "try again, but concentrate on playing the ghost notes quieter". I didn't realise I did this until I asked one of my students to play something again one day and he just kept looking at me expectantly. When I eventually said "Why haven't you started?", he said "well you usually give me a little pep talk first to tell me what I need to do differently". When I thought about this I was really pleased so now always do it consciously. Just be careful to only point out one or two things to focus on at a time. If there are a number of mistakes then you can't correct everything at the same time, your student won't be able to take in all the information and remember it as they play through (also it might discourage them if they think they're doing nothing right). Choose one or two of the main issues and concentrate on those initially, then as these improve, you can point out any other things that need attention.

Communication

Communication with your students is important. We communicate our ideas to them through a mixture of words and demonstration. Try to make the lesson an interaction between the two of you rather than just you talking at your pupil. Frequently asking questions of your students can help make sure you're both contributing equally to the lesson and also helps with the idea of not spoon-feeding.

Talk to students at their level and make sure you use words they'll understand. In life you wouldn't talk to a 7 year old the same way you would to a 15 year old or a 40 year old and it's the same in teaching. Both what you say and the way you say it will be different for each individual depending on their age, maturity and other factors (including if you're teaching someone whose first language isn't English), so make sure to consider this for each pupil. This might be obvious, but don't talk too fast (this is something I have to be really careful of myself, the only person I know who talks faster than me is my sister!) and don't mumble. Some new or shy students might be afraid to say they haven't heard you properly. Don't just assume they've understood you, sometimes you might need to explain something in a different way. You can often tell from a student's facial expressions if they haven't got a clue what you're talking about! Be particularly careful of this with new students; once you get used to each other it'll be easier for you to realise if they've not understood and how best to explain things to them. Sometimes students might be reluctant to tell you that they still don't understand if you've already tried explaining something to them in two or three different ways as it might make them feel stupid. If your student's struggling, ask them questions to make sure they've understood exactly what they should be doing.

Demonstrate things to your students when necessary. If a picture is worth a thousand words, then someone right next to you showing you what to do is surely worth a whole lot more. As with talking, demonstrate things slowly and point out any important bits. The fact that your student can both see and hear what you're doing is a huge help. Do try to avoid showing off though, remember it's about them, not you. That being said, it's occasionally worth putting the odd short tasty fill or hi-hat variation in for new students just to show them you're a good player and give them something to aspire to. Just make sure that with existing students you get the right balance between inspiring them and not being self-indulgent.

A big part of communication with your students is encouragement. Students of all ages and abilities need to build confidence and your encouragement and confirmation of their abilities helps massively. Use positive language and be sure to pick out things they've done well, as well as things that they need to improve upon, especially with younger and beginner pupils. With more advanced and experienced students, elements of mentoring come into play to help guide them in their career, reach their potential and have the confidence they need to succeed.

Body language plays a part in communication too. There's nothing worse than negative body language from a teacher. If you look bored, tired or generally like you don't want to be there, then this is highly discouraging for students (and rude) and is likely to rub off on them. Positive body language like smiling, nodding, making eye contact and generally looking alert however can really help to encourage and engage your students.

Targets and Goals

It's important to set a mixture of short and long-term goals and targets for your students. This gives them something to aim for and can encourage them as it shows their progression. In the short term, a goal might be to play a certain beat for a certain amount of time. For example, I might tell a student when we're learning new beats that the goal is to play the beat for 30 seconds before we can move on to the next one (I tend to think if they can play it fluently for 30 seconds, they can play it for 3 minutes). Then they know when they're practising at home to aim for playing the beat for at least 30 seconds without stopping. A longer-term target might be aiming to play one-handed 16th notes on the hi-hat at a certain tempo (so they can play songs like Coldplay's *Paradise* or James Brown's *Funky Drummer*). It can take time to work on technique and improve speed, so this will be a more long-term goal.

I'll refer more to this in another section, but if you're in a country where graded exams are popular, then for certain students, setting a target of passing a certain grade within a certain timescale or with a certain mark can also help them focus their practice.

You can see how having specific targets and goals can focus students. It gives them a sense of achievement and enjoyment and I've found it helps them want to practise more rather than meandering along. Communicating well, making sure they're not afraid to make mistakes and coaching your students to help them work things out for themselves will also help make you a much more effective teacher.

How to Teach - Specific

We've talked in general terms about teaching. Coaching pupils and not spoon-feeding, communicating, demonstrating and setting targets. But let's get down to the nitty gritty of how to teach some specific drum examples.

Before even thinking about playing a drum, you're going to have to show your student how to hold the sticks. Some of you might never have really thought about how you hold your sticks. Perhaps you were shown in your very first lesson or if you're self-taught, do what you've seen on videos or what feels right to you. This is where I think teaching is great for every drummer as it actually makes you analyse what you do, especially technically, and can make you a much better player as a result. Look where the stick is in relation to your fingers and work out how to explain this to your students. For example, while there are a number of other perfectly good grips, I play matched grip with first finger fulcrum (the fulcrum is the pivot point, really important for stick rebound). The stick goes between my thumb and first finger, first joint (fulcrum), I gently wrap the other fingers round the stick then turn my wrist so the knuckle of my first finger is the highest point of my hand. I also have a couple of centimetres of stick coming out of the back of my hand. This is how I explain my grip to students. Obviously it's a lot easier when you're actually showing them, but you get the important points (you can see a video lesson of this at: *www.YouTube.com/brocksterdrums*). As I've said before, you may use another equally good grip, I'm just suggesting certain things to think about with regards to describing it to someone else.

Common issues I find are the students holding the stick too tight, not having any stick out the back of their hand (if there's some markings/words on their sticks that happen to be in the same place as their thumb for example, I tell them to always look for that when holding their sticks) and pointing their first finger up the stick towards the tip rather than gently wrapping it round the stick. Once you've sorted these issues, it's all about flicking from their wrists and getting a good rebound off the drum.

Let's take the classic 8 beat that everyone knows, quite possibly the first drum beat you learnt (if you don't know what I mean, I'm talking AC/DC *Back in Black*). It's certainly always the first or second beat I teach. But how to teach it? Well, I usually start with using a counting system, either 1,2,3,4 or 1+2+3+4+ (probably the first if I was teaching it without the notation, but for me preferably the second and use notation). Get your student to cross their sticks/hands over first. Play continuous notes on the hi-hat with their right hand (using the tip of the stick) and count 1+2+3+4+ as they play them (I'd notate these as 8th notes). When your student is comfortable playing that, get them to add the bass drum on counts 1 and 3. Doing it from notated music, I'd ask them what we've added in this beat and hopefully they'll say the bass drum. If not, I'd prompt them by saying well, it's written in the bottom space, so it'll be the lowest sounding drum in the kit (again this is about trying to help them work things out for themselves). When they've got that sorted, I'll take the bass drum notes out and get them to add the Snare on 2 and 4 instead (again, seeing if they can work it out from notation). Once they've got that going, we'll slowly try to put all the elements (bass, snare, hi-hats) together.

Next comes the bit where your teaching skills really come in. Hopefully your student will be a fast learner with great co-ordination and will get the hang of it straight away, but a lot of the time they won't, so what can you do to help them if they're struggling? These ideas are useful for teaching any beat, not just this one. Obviously it will depend on what specifically they're struggling with, but here are some ideas.

First of all, get them to try playing the beat slowly (quite often students try and take things too fast, too soon). Also, they don't need to play the beat repeatedly straight away. You could get them to play it just once initially, then when they can do that correctly each time they can try it twice in a row and only when they can do that try looping it round repeatedly for as long as possible (as mentioned earlier, about 30 seconds). Remind your student that all the +'s are just hi-hats, so after each bass and snare there'll be a hi-hat by itself. You can also get them to try different words if counting isn't helping. For example "Bass and Snare and Bass and Snare and", or the ever popular "Boots 'n Cats 'n

Boots 'n Cats 'n". If they're still struggling I'd break the beat down into smaller sections. So first of all get them playing the first two notes, bass and hi-hat together followed by just a hi-hat. After they're comfortable doing that then add snare and hi-hat together after those two notes. Then add just a hi-hat at the end etc.

While this basic 8 beat is something we can do in our sleep, remember it's one of the first things your student's learning and some people find the co-ordination element takes time initially.

Reading

Being English and learning piano and french horn before the drums, I was brought up calling rhythms crotchets, quavers, semiquavers etc. so don't readily use the terms ¼ note, 8th note and 16th note myself. However, I do tell my students that rhythms can be known by either term and for the purpose of this book have gone with 8th note etc. to make it easier for people to understand, whatever country they live in.

When teaching students to read I usually start off by teaching each rhythm on the snare drum first before using it in beats and fills. I start one rhythm at a time and don't move on to the next until they can read each one fluently. I always relate words to each rhythm. This helps when a student's learning a rhythm for the first time as it gives them a sound/pattern to associate it with. The most common words I use are:

Tea (¼ note)
Coffee (group of two 8th notes)
Coca-Cola (group of four 16th notes)
Apple Pie (two 16th notes followed by an 8th note)
Blackcurrant (an 8th note followed by two 16th notes)

For a pdf of this and other counting systems with the rhythms written out go to:
www.how2teachdrums.com/reading

The above are what I was taught by my drum teacher and are what I use the vast majority of the time, but occasionally I use other words. You can choose whatever words you and your students want (as long as the words have the right amount of syllables to fit the rhythms obviously!). If your student's really into football (soccer!) you could use football team names. Instead of Tea, Coffee, Coca-Cola, Apple Pie and Blackcurrant you could go with Spurs, Chelsea, Crystal Palace, Liverpool and Man City.

Of course you can also count using 1e+a, 2e+a, 3e+a, 4e+a. This can be a helpful counting system as students will know which beat of the bar the rhythm's on. Different students find different things helpful, but I often find words as opposed to 1e+a type counting are better for younger beginner students (possibly because they're easier to process and remember). Adults however sometimes find 1e+a most suitable as they can understand the counting better in a mathematical way. I tend to make sure that from an intermediate level onwards students are aware of both types of counting so they can choose whichever helps them best in a given situation.

When teaching students to read beats I often tell them to think of it as a grid system. If the hi-hats are playing continuous 8th notes then work out where everything else fits in relation to those hi-hats. This can particularly help when reading beats with 16th note bass and snare drums.

Troubleshooting

We touched on this when talking about teaching a basic 8 beat, but troubleshooting (knowing how to help students when they're struggling with something) is one of the things that makes a good teacher. Lots of drummers could suggest which beats might be good for a student to learn, but how many of them will know different ways of helping the student play the beat if they're finding it difficult? Breaking things down into smaller sections and slowing them down are always a good place to start if students are struggling. These are the main things that I usually try first and often this is enough to sort things out. I also make sure students know that this is the best way to work on things they're having difficulty with so they can do this when practising at home. Playing just the hands or just the feet, then gradually re-introducing the other limbs can also help if it's a co-ordination issue.

Obviously every situation and student is different depending on specifically what's going wrong. As mentioned earlier, when reading beats from notation thinking of it as a grid system can often help. If they know for example, that all the hi-hats are 8th notes but can hear they aren't playing them all at an equal speed then they must be doing something wrong.

Encouraging students to count or concentrate on keeping a steady pulse can sometimes be useful, as can demonstrating to them so they can hear exactly how something should sound. It might be that you just need to explain something in a different way. Look at a student's technique, is there something they're doing technically wrong that's stopping them from being able to play something correctly? Sometimes when looking at a students hands you can see that there's something not symmetrical and this may be a pointer towards a technical issue (often their weaker hand holding the stick slightly differently). Perhaps they're not starting their sticks at different heights when trying to play flams.

There are numerous reasons why a particular beat, fill or rhythm might cause a student problems and it's your job to work out exactly what that is. The moment when they've worked through the problems and can finally play something can be really pleasing and worthwhile for you both.

Vocalising and Clapping

Using sounds aside from the drum kit like vocalising or clapping can be really useful. Vocalising can work well if a pupil's struggling in beats or fills. Boom, Ba, Boom Boom, Ba or Gung, Ga, Gung Gung, Ga could be a way of vocalising a simple beat (almost like beat boxing but with a less realistic sound). I'm always singing beats to my students, it means they're focusing on the actual sound of the beat rather than trying to work out which bass drum goes with which hi-hat. It also means I don't necessarily need to get them to move off the kit, I can just say, let's play this beat and sing it to my student rather than having to continually swap places with them. I actively encourage them to sing the beat they're playing in their head at all times as they play it. I find it helps them groove more and eliminates some mistakes. If they're about to play the wrong snare pattern, but are singing the correct one in their head, this can help stop them from making that mistake.

Clapping can be handy too. When teaching snare rhythms I'll often get a student to put the sticks down and clap a section if they're having problems. It means they're focusing on the rhythm without the distraction of holding the sticks, thinking about which sticking to use and hearing the loud sound of the drum. You clapping the pulse during beats can be a big help if your student's getting faster or slower, it acts like a metronome (you could also click your sticks together for this).

Teaching Fills

There are a number of different ways to teach fills. There might be a particular way you were taught (if you can remember!) that you want to try, or you might have some ideas of your own. I'm going to share one way I find myself using quite a lot to help beginners learn to play fills. I do teach students to read fills from written notation, but it's really important for them to learn to make up their own. They not only need to learn where to start fills and how to end them, but have a system to help them be creative and not get into the habit of playing the same old fills all the time.

I tend to start off by working on whole bar fills (talking in 4/4), then move on to half bar fills (which depending on style are often more usable) later, once students are comfortable with whole bar fills. We initially work in 4 bar chunks. I explain to pupils that songs are often in 8/12/16 bar sections so they might not eventually want to add fills so regularly, but by working in 4 bar sections it not only helps their counting but also means they'll be playing the fills, which are ultimately the focus, more frequently. As it's 4 bars, I'll get students playing 3 bars of beat followed by one bar of fill.

I start by getting them to play my absolute most hated drum fill (Tré Cool can occasionally get away with it in Green Day, but that's about it!). This is going round the drums clockwise starting with the snare, playing "Coca-Cola" (a group of 4 16th notes) on each drum. Presuming you're working on a standard kit with snare and three toms, playing this rhythm once on each drum will add up to a bar of 4 beats.

Once they can play 3 bars of beat followed by this fill we then talk about adding the Crash cymbal. This is one way of explaining and introducing it. We add the Crash at the beginning of the first beat, immediately after the fill. It's basically played instead of the very first hi-hat note. We initially practise playing just the first beat with the Crash at the beginning and then add the remaining bars of beat and fill. I explain that using the Crash cymbal is a little bit like using a capital letter when writing. When we finish writing a sentence, we put a full stop and then always start the next sentence with a capital letter. The Crash cymbal is like this capital letter. We come to the end of a section of a song, add our fill and then start the next section with our Crash cymbal. Once they've grasped this, from this point on we'll always be playing 3 bars of beat, 1 bar of fill and then adding the Crash when we return to the beginning.

The next stage is to start changing the order of the drums in the fill. Your students will still be using the rhythm "Coca-Cola", but rather than playing it clockwise round the drums, get them to play the rhythm once on each drum but vary the order they play the drums in. If each time they get to the fill they play the drums in a different order, this already makes each fill sound a little different and stops your students getting into the habit of always going round the drums in the same order.

The next step is to introduce one more rhythm, "Coffee". Students can then mix up the rhythms "Coffee" and "Coca-Cola" in any combination they like. For example:

Coca-Cola, Coffee, Coca-Cola, Coffee

Coffee, Coffee, Coca-Cola, Coffee

Coca-Cola, Coca-Cola, Coffee, Coffee

As long as students play each rhythm/word on a different drum, making sure to play one on each of the snare and 3 toms, then they will always get a 4 beat (and therefore whole bar) fill.

The next stage is to add two more rhythms, "Apple Pie" and "Blackcurrant" (obviously use whatever counting system you've been using to teach reading, so if you've gone with different words or counting, then use those instead). You can then use the four rhythms your students have learnt in any order or combination (you don't have to use every rhythm, every time), for example:

Blackcurrant, Coffee, Coca-Cola, Coffee

Coffee, Coca-Cola, Apple Pie, Coca-Cola

Coca-Cola, Coca-Cola, Blackcurrant, Apple Pie

The ultimate aim for this initial fill learning stage is for students to be able to play any combination of the rhythms "Coffee", "Coca-Cola", "Apple Pie" and "Blackcurrant" they choose, going round the drums in a different order each time. There are literally hundreds of possible combinations. This also means that from the early stages of learning fills students are getting used to being creative and making up their own combinations rather than just copying a few fills they've learnt from you by rote.

As mentioned earlier, the next step would be for students to learn to play half bar fills. You use the same concept as above, but get students playing 3 and a half bars of beat followed by a half bar (two beat) fill. This means they will just use two words/rhythms in the fill. Often it's not the fill that causes problems here, but the fact that they have to learn to count half a bar of beat.

So far we've talked about always playing each rhythm on just one drum. Next, get your students to split some rhythms between drums. "Apple Pie" could then be played for example with the first two notes on one drum and the third on another (this works great at the end of a two beat fill) and "Coca-Cola" could be played with each of its four notes on a different drum (doing this clockwise round the kit is something Chad Smith sometimes does at the end of fills).

As time goes on there are numerous other things to do with fills. The fills we've talked about so far are mainly for simple rock, pop and funk style playing. When you introduce new styles always make sure students learn to play appropriate fills too. Another thing to do with fills over time is to add rudiments. Paradiddles, flams and 6 strokes rolls always work a treat as do bounce doubles. Linear fills are good for more advanced students, when introducing both feet and working with groupings of 3's and 5's, you can create some great fusion fills.

Group Teaching

I'll be honest, I personally prefer one-to-one tuition, but in case you do find yourself teaching groups, here's a few things to consider (mainly referring to groups of two). I know some teachers of instruments like trumpet and clarinet that regularly teach groups of two students. Those students will each have their own instrument so can play either separately or together in lessons. It's pretty unusual however that you'll have two drum kits in your teaching room, so you'll have to think very carefully about how to keep the pupil that's not on the kit at any given time involved. Getting students to critique one another's performances by saying one thing that was good and one thing that could be better can be good as it means the other pupil is listening and being analytical. By making sure they say one good thing as well as one that could be better they're being both encouraging and constructive. Getting the student who isn't at the kit to click their sticks and act like a metronome for the other is also a useful option. You could perhaps consider having a practice pad for them so they can play along and practise the correct rhythms even when they're not at the kit. Swap the students round regularly so each one's not off the kit for too long at a time. If there happens to be congas or bongos in your teaching room then the pupil not at the kit could always jam along on those too.

Getting the students playing patterns for each other to copy (also sometimes called "call and response") at the start of the lesson can be a good warm up. For beginners, playing simple snare duets can be helpful as they each have a part to play and it gets them used to playing with others. It also improves their sense of pulse and musical awareness.

The real challenge of group teaching, aside from keeping both students involved throughout the lesson, is that each student has their own strengths and weaknesses and will progress at different rates. You need to make sure that both are challenged and learning equally from the lesson. The time may come when you might have to switch the groups round (if you're teaching more than one group) or change to individual lessons.

Finally, make sure you write down separately for each pupil what they need to practise and anything specific they need to focus on.

Practice

One thing that plays a big part in your students continual improvement as drummers is practice. To a certain extent, this is out of your hands. It's up to your students to spend their own time practising and the more time they put in, generally, the quicker they'll improve. There are however a few ways in which you can help. The first is by encouraging them to practice as much as possible. Talk to each student about the importance of practising in their first lesson and be sure to encourage them in lessons when you can tell that the time they've spent practising has made a difference. I try to explain that practising regularly is much better than suddenly trying to cram in an hour the night before their lesson, by which point some of the improvements they made in their lesson the week before might well be forgotten.

The amount of time you suggest your students should spend practising will differ from student to student depending on a number of factors, but do try to get each student into a practice routine. This way practice becomes a habit. I also make a point of encouraging students to play along to music at home and not only practise just what I've told them to. Jamming with friends or joining a band can be great too. Not only will it be enjoyable for your students, but it will help them become more rounded drummers and give them the opportunity to actually use the various beats and fills they've been learning.

The second thing is making sure your students know exactly what they're supposed to be practising each week. If you just say as the lesson goes along, "have a little look at that bit at home", then in my experience they can often forget. Make sure you write down exactly what they're supposed to be working on (in a notebook of theirs, or on the page of music you're working on) for the following week's lesson along with any specific areas to be careful of, or any helpful tips. For example, to concentrate on a certain bar number, to not slow down in a certain section, or technical comments to do with a student's grip (this one I often find myself doing for beginners). If you're not entirely sure your student understands what they're supposed to be practising then ask them to clarify with you at the end of the lesson.

The third is something we've already covered, spoon-feeding (or the lack of it)! By not spoon-feeding your students, but instead helping them to work things out for themselves whilst pointing them in the right direction, you're teaching them skills that they can use both in lessons and when practising alone. If a student's struggling with something you've given them to practice at home, but in lessons you've taught them how to break things into smaller sections, slow things down and they can also read well, then they're a lot more capable of working through any problems and spending their practice time constructively. If however, you always demonstrate everything to your students first in lessons and always point out their mistakes before giving them a little time to work out where and when they're going wrong themselves, then your students aren't used to thinking independently. They might then struggle to identify and rectify any mistakes they're making when they're practising.

My final thought on practising comes courtesy of my mum and sister. When I was talking to my sister about certain elements of this book she said that she remembers a comment my mum made to her when she was learning the clarinet as a teenager (she seems to recall needing lots of encouragement to practise!). "You don't practise until you've got it right, you practise until you can't get it wrong". Says it all. Not just a pretty face my mum!

Lesson Structure

It's important to give some thought to how you're going to structure your lessons. I'll give you an idea of how I would generally structure a 30 minute lesson (lessons for advanced students and via Skype tend to be longer but this is by far my most common length for beginner/intermediate students). To start with I always do a short warm-up of anything up to 5 minutes (discussed in more detail in the next section). I then tend to split the remaining time into doing two separate activities. When possible, I make them quite different. One for example, might be something technical or notation-based like working on bounce doubles or working on some rhythm reading, whilst the other might be learning to play the beats of a specific song (and playing these beats along to the song when they're ready). I tend to do the more 'fun' element second - leave them happy! At the end of the lesson, verbally recap what you've covered and make sure they know what to practise for the next lesson.

Warm Ups

I explain to my students that it's like sport. You wouldn't (or shouldn't) start without doing some form of stretches or warm-up first because you might get injured, and it's the same with drumming. This might involve one of the following: rudiments, co-ordination exercises, getting better dexterity round the kit. But they'll ALWAYS start slowly and then possibly get faster at some point. You can make up loads of your own ideas and get students to create their own too. It can often be a good way of working on certain areas like rudiments and playing to a click. I encourage students to always start with a warm up at home too, there's no point only doing it in lessons. Don't forget the feet when doing warm ups. I think people often focus on the hands, but it's pretty simple to add something like quarter notes (or as they get more advanced a samba pattern) in the feet underneath hand exercises, then everything's warmed up and you've chucked a bit of co-ordination in too.

First Lesson

Whether teaching in person or online it's always worth having a bit of a chat with your student in their first lesson. Probably less so with younger beginners because they don't tend to have such developed musical tastes or much of an idea of what they hope to achieve other than liking the sound of drums and wanting to play them (this isn't always the case though, so do ask). They can also sometimes be a little shyer at this age while they're getting to know you so too many questions can be a bit scary and if they're not sure what to say or don't have an answer they can get discouraged.

Find out any specific targets your new students have ("I've always wanted to play *When The Levee Breaks*"). If they already play ask about previous drumming experience they might have, if they've had lessons before and why they've decided to start learning with you. The first lesson for people who are already drummers will often be a lot about you asking them to play various things and find out what level they're at. Can they read drum music? Do they know their rudiments?

Are they left or right handed? I tend to start all beginner drummers on a right handed kit. Most left handers soon get into the habit of leading fills with their right hand etc. and it can even be helpful for intricate snare ghost notes as they're doing this with their dominant hand, where for right handers it's their weaker hand. I tend to do this as it's easier for students in the future if they're doing kit share gigs. However, if it becomes clear that playing the kit right handed is affecting their progress then we turn the kit round and go left handed (I think I've only ever done this with two students, it took them a couple of weeks to get used to it, but they've never looked back). There's also a lot of amusement to be had when they get more advanced (if you're right handed) as you have to demonstrate things to these students on a left handed kit! I've actually found this quite fun and it can only be a good thing for your own playing and co-ordination.

Ask new students what their favourite genres and bands are. You can then use these songs for them to play along with and can also teach them some of the beats when they're at a suitable ability level. Stress to students that the more they practise and play drums generally outside of lessons, the better they'll be and the quicker they'll generally progress. I find out what, if anything, they have to practise on and discuss what they need to buy if necessary.

Specialising

Most teachers tend to find themselves teaching a lot of beginners, mostly teenagers and probably a lot of rock songs! Certainly when you're starting out I'd imagine you'll find yourself teaching a high percentage of these types of students and it's probably best to think a fair amount about what you want to teach them early on (as discussed in our *Drumming Timeline*). It'll be a great way to cut your teeth and whilst I probably most enjoy teaching advanced students who practise hard and learn so much themselves, there's also great pleasure to be taken in giving students a really solid start as a drummer and watching them grow. However, as you get more experienced you might decide you want to specialise in certain areas. Perhaps there's a gap in the market in your area or you feel there's something you enjoy teaching and is a particular strength of yours.

There are some teachers who only teach advanced players, but these are usually people who have made a name for themselves already and aspiring pros go to them because of who they are. You're unlikely to fall into this category right now, but if it's what you want to do and you've got the relevant knowledge and skills, then get a long term plan and go for it. Perhaps you're a great double pedal player, this is definitely an area where you could market yourself as a teacher. Pupils into Metal often really want to get into double pedal playing, but while many teachers might be able to show pupils a few things on double pedals (I'm not one!), there'll be few who are really good at it. The same goes for jazz, teaching adults and Latin amongst other things. I'm not necessarily suggesting you market yourself solely in these specialised areas as it's unlikely (although not impossible) to get you a huge number of pupils initially. However, as well as your standard adverts (which as we'll discuss later you should target to a certain extent) you should put out ads for your specific skill too. If it's double pedal, put some ads in metal music/drummers forums, classifieds etc. Do a couple of YouTube videos of you nailing your double bass or jazz stuff to show that you know what you're doing and link to them from the adverts (you can also pick up students directly from YouTube if you write your title, description and tags properly). The one area where you might be able to get a higher proportion of work from specialising is online drum lessons. You've got so many more potential students when teaching via Skype that specialising is a genuine option.

What Your Student Wants to Learn

As we've discussed, it's vital to think about what you want to teach and how you want to teach it. However, it's a two way street between you and your student, and each will want something different (to be honest this is one of the things that always keeps teaching interesting, no two students are the same). As mentioned, talk to new pupils in their first lesson about why they want to play drums and if there's anything in particular they want to learn or any specific goals they have. I often find younger students just want to "play drums", so you follow your *Drumming Timeline* and along the way they'll develop certain interests which you can start to include.

Every student who comes to me as a beginner will learn the basics of technique, reading, beats, aural, timekeeping etc. and follow my *Drumming Timeline*, with a slant towards any specifics goals they may have. Then when they've reached a certain level we can focus more on the styles/areas that they want to learn (this is called pupil-led learning and is currently popular in the teaching of various subjects in schools). If students have a solid drumming foundation, then whether they want to focus on rock, metal, reggae, jazz etc. at a later stage, it will make everything easier.

One exception to this rule to a certain extent is when I've taught adults who want initially to take a short course of lessons so they can play a certain song, or a few beats and fills to get them started. Although even then they still need to be taught the basics of technique and timekeeping etc., this is the one time when I may spend a little less time on certain elements, such as reading. Another possible exception are students who might have played for a while already but come saying they want to be more comfortable with fills or have better technique (they might feel it's getting in the way of them progressing or they are getting pain due to bad technique). There are so many different reasons people want to have lessons and they're paying you to teach them, so it's important to find out their exact needs and goals in order to keep them happy and motivated and give them what they're paying for. However, I do think it's important to have certain personal standards. For example, if a beginner came to me and said "I want to learn but not read", I'd say no! (Unless they had specific educational needs that might make that a serious issue). Or, "I don't like rudiments, can we just play to songs." Again, I'd say no, however I always try to make rudiments interesting and relevant. They're a great way to work on technique but use them in fills and get students to try different combinations of drums. They're only boring if you make them that way! There's no reason why you can't work on lots of different skills at once, for example adding feet underneath rudiments and getting pupils to play them along to music. This way you're also working on aural, four-way co-ordination and timekeeping skills whilst making the initial rudiment more interesting and relevant.

I occasionally get students who think that when they've played a beat once they can move on to the next and I'll stress that that's just the start. The beat needs to be fluent and sound good. Then they need to be able to play it continuously and add fills (and then come out of the fill and play the beat correctly the very first time - usually where they go wrong!).

What I'm saying is that lessons are a two-way street and your focus and approach should be different depending on each student's needs, interests and goals. Don't rigidly stick to using only material from your *Drumming Timeline* just for the sake of it. However, there are some things that to me are really important for all students to learn and if they're not happy learning those things, then the bottom line for me is they can learn with someone else. For me it's about integrity.

What Experience Do I Need?

Now you have some idea of what to teach and how to teach it, you should be feeling much more confident about drum teaching, but you still might be unsure as to what experience you need and wondering if you're ready to start. There's no one straightforward answer to this. It probably depends on what exactly you're wanting to do. I guess one simplistic answer is that if you know more than someone else about drumming, then there's something you can teach them. That doesn't necessarily mean you're ready to be a drum teacher though.

If you're looking to work for a music service or a school, they might require specific qualifications, for example a music degree. If on the other hand you're just setting up as a one man/woman outfit (which is most likely how you'll start), then there are no requirements. This is both a good and a bad thing. It makes drum teaching an option accessible to any good drummer regardless of their educational background which is good, but it can also mean you get some bad drum teachers who are ripping people off, giving pupils bad habits and teaching little more than a few beats and fills that students play ad-infinitum. Their pupils have no real knowledge or technique base and little prospect of advancing far unless they're naturally very talented and inquisitive. I'm guessing that as you're taking the time to read this book then you're intending to be a good drum teacher!

Everyone has to start somewhere, to give their first drum lesson. Work out your *Drumming Timeline* and just get stuck in. Start teaching a couple of people and see how it goes. You'll soon start to figure out what works and what doesn't, which areas you're confident with and those that need more thought. To get started and give it a go you could offer one of your musician mates a lesson swap. You teach them the drums if they'll teach you the bass (cue bass player jokes!). It'll be good for you to practise teaching and you'll get something in exchange. Currently a couple of my advanced high school students (aged 17 and

18) have each started teaching a pupil. One is teaching a friend and another someone who lives down their road. I've given them some ideas and pointers, and they're really enjoying learning how to teach, and earning some pocket money in the process.

Experience is something you gain over time and you'll constantly be improving and honing your teaching style, but here are a number of attributes that it would be useful to have:

Good communication skills
Listening skills
Adaptability
Ability to read drum music
Good knowledge of drum parts in songs (including what's popular right now)
Sense of humour
Solid technique
Good drummer (gigging standard)
Professionalism
Good organisation skills
Punctual
Patient
Observant

It's very unlikely you'll have every single one, but if you haven't got the majority of them or aren't prepared to work on improving the ones that aren't currently your strengths, you might want to consider whether drum teaching's really for you.

Where to Teach

Y ou might be thinking ok, I've now got an idea of what I want to teach, but where can I teach? Drums are a big, noisy instrument, you can't teach them just anywhere.

At Your Home

Some of us are lucky enough to have a space at home where our drums are set up, there are no noise issues and there's room enough for you and your student to move round the kit. Great! An obvious advantage of teaching at home is that you don't need to travel anywhere, which cuts down on expenses and even more importantly, time. For example, if you're teaching four 30 minute lessons one evening at your house, if you book them one after another, that's 2 hours. If you have to travel between different locations for each lesson, it could easily take twice as long (and you won't be getting twice the money).

One note of caution. Chances are you'll probably be teaching a lot of children or teenagers (mostly strangers), so there are some child protection issues to think about. There's a little more info on this later in the book, but in short, as far as "where shall I teach" goes, I strongly recommend teaching in a room that has a window in it (or some glass in the door). When teaching at your home, don't teach in a bedroom. Ideally you wouldn't teach in a bedroom at students' houses either, but this often isn't possible or practical as lots of pupils have their kits in their room. If this is the case, then at least leave the door ajar.

At The Pupil's Home

You should consider charging more if you're a 'mobile' teacher. As mentioned above, it takes you time and fuel to travel to pupils' houses, and people are prepared to pay a little more for the convenience. The issues of space and noise are the pupil's problem, not yours. Plus, if you're lucky, you'll get made a cup of coffee and offered a biscuit too! (When I used to travel to pupils' houses, I even got given dinner a couple of times).

In a Music Shop

Lots of music shops offer music tuition. It could be a general musical instrument shop or a drum store. They often have the space and equipment already and by offering lessons, they're getting more potential customers into their shop. They're likely to charge you a small amount for the use of their space so make sure you factor this into your pricing. Draw up a list of your local shops and get in touch with them - email and phone are fine, but why not make a bit of an effort and pop into the shop and have a chat with them face-to-face. Do your research first so you know whether they offer lessons already on any instruments at all, this will make you seem more serious about wanting to teach at their shop.

Rehearsal Studio

The same applies as for music shops, they've got the space and equipment, so get in touch.

Schools/Music Services

If you work for a school or music service then it will be their responsibility to sort out a room for you complete with drum kit etc. Don't be afraid to if say it's too small though. I've taught in a number of schools and the rooms are generally fine, but occasionally you might find yourself put in a room so small you can't swing a cat in it, let alone squeeze in a drum kit and two people! If the room really is too small, then do say, it's not fair on you or your students, let alone their ears. Either way, make sure you wear your earplugs (but you'd do this anyway, right....?)

Agencies

Google "music lesson agency", "home music lessons" or "music lessons" in your area to see if there are any agencies locally you could start teaching for. Parents sometimes like going through an agency (rightly or wrongly depending on the whether the agency's any good) because they might not be sure what to look for in a drum teacher and feel you've been vetted in some way (teaching-wise and for child protection). If there aren't any agencies in your area, how about setting one up? Get together a list of drum, guitar, bass, piano, singing teachers etc. and put a website together. There are a number of different ways you could choose to administer this financially, but a simple way would be to charge the parents a small one-off fee for you introducing them to the teacher. Or, charge the teachers a one-off fee for each pupil you provide them with. Or, charge them both! Just make sure you only use good teachers as you want to build a good reputation.

What to Teach On

N ow you've thought about where to teach, there are a few other considerations too. What to teach on? Well, drums obviously, but more specifically what about practice kits and electronic kits? Personally, I'd avoid teaching beginners on a practice kit. I had a lesson with a highly respected teacher once who taught on a practise kit at his home. Excellent lesson, but the kit only worked because I already knew how to play. Whether there was sound from the kit or decent rebound didn't matter so much, we were more talking about ideas and concepts. (In fact we did very little playing and talked for a very long time whilst drinking strong coffee; he had some great advice and stories).

Electronic Drums

If you're not teaching beginners or are teaching Skype lessons, electronic drums can be great. Having the in-built metronome can be helpful, volume becomes less of an issue (for you, the student and any possible neighbours) and the fact that you can plug ipods, usb etc. into the back of most electronic kits makes playing along to music really easy. One word of caution though. Rebound and getting a good sound out of the kit are really important for beginners. If you're teaching beginners and intend to use an electronic kit, make sure it's got a mesh type head on the snare, not one of the rubber pads. Getting good, solid stick technique is vital for beginners and getting the right rebound off the drum is a big part of that. Only mesh heads on an electronic kit can really do this (the vast majority of the Roland kits have mesh snare heads). The one thing that you can't really teach on an electronic kit is sound/timbre (unless you're talking high end, expensive gear). On an acoustic kit, students can hear the minute differences (again, particularly with the snare) that for example, not playing in the centre of the drum makes and concentrate on getting a good musical tone. Things like playing the hi-hats with the right bit of the stick and in the right place when playing beats. If teaching beginners on an electronic kit is your only option, then don't let these things stop you, but do be aware of them. Perhaps you could use just an acoustic snare to play basic rudiments and rhythms on sometimes when starting these students. This'll help get them into good habits that will then stick with them whether they continue onto an electronic or acoustic kit.

Playback Facilities

One other thing to consider is playback facilities. As mentioned a few times in this book, it's a must for students to play to music as often as possible. Drums are very much an ensemble instrument so this really helps their listening skills at the same time as developing a student's inner clock. To make my life easier, I've got all my drumless backing tracks, click tracks (ranging from very slow to really fast at 5bpm intervals) and a huge load of songs and albums on an mp3 player. This means that whenever I'm teaching I've got all the tracks I need with me. I'd strongly recommend this if possible. It's then also really easy to download tracks and put them on your mp3 player when students have songs they bring to you that they want to learn. You could do the same with a laptop too, but it's bigger to carry round and worth more if it's stolen or damaged.

Drums being a rather loud instrument, it's important you have reasonably powerful speakers. I've found the best scenario is that you have a PA system to play CDs or an mp3 player through. For a number of reasons this isn't always possible or practical though, so there are other options. If you're using an electronic kit, it's usually possible to plug an mp3 player into that. Another option is getting a headphone splitter and two pairs of headphones (one for you, one for your student) to plug into your mp3 player. You might find yourself constantly battling with wire spaghetti as I call it (I swear headphone cables like to have a party in your bag!), but this is a really good option when you're travelling and doing mobile teaching as funnily enough, there aren't that many students with PA's set up at home! As wireless headphones get cheaper this might make life easier. If you're teaching from your home studio you might of course have all your tracks on your computer or laptop which would work really well too as long as you're running it through powerful speakers. Just be aware of your students' ears and don't go too loud with the volume though.

When teaching online via Skype it's important to make sure that both you and your student can hear any click or track that they're playing to. This means two things. Firstly that they can't be listening to the music on just headphones as you need to hear both their drumming and the song. Secondly, the music must be played their end, not yours. There's a very slight delay when using Skype which makes it pointless for them to play along to music that's coming from your side of the feed. They'd hear it slightly later than you do, so their playing would always sound late to you making this totally unworkable. Basically, as far as students playing to music when teaching online goes, any music needs to be coming out of speakers their end.

What Equipment Do Your Students Need?

What do your students need when they start having drum lessons? Well this partly depends on where you're teaching them. If you're teaching them over Skype or at their house then they'll need their own kit for lessons (although I have taught a more advanced student via Skype with just a practice pad, which worked well for technique and rudiment based work). If however, they're having lessons at your studio or at school then to start with it's fine for students to have just a pair of sticks (5A's are generally a good model for beginners) and a practice pad. It would also be useful for them to have a metronome. This actually makes starting drums very inexpensive compared to other instruments as drumsticks and a practice pad are relatively cheap and there's a number of free metronome apps available for phones and tablets. It means students can work on technique at home to start with and then upgrade to a drum kit once they know they're enjoying drum lessons and want to continue.

This is where it's worth doing some research into starter kits and electronic kits. Most students and/or their parents know little about drum kits when starting out so will likely turn to you for advice. It's important that you know what's available and suitable for them and at what price (as opposed to just knowing about the mid-range and top of the line kits which you're more likely to own). Firstly, there are a lot of rubbish starter kits available on eBay made by companies that you've never heard of where the cymbals dent after 5 minutes and the threads on the hardware go in no time at all. These might initially seem appealing to some students because of their low price, but steer them well clear as the kits are little more than toys. They'll thank you for it in the end. There are however, a few really good starter kits out there made by reputable companies at a price range suitable for a student's first kit. Starter kits normally come with everything the student needs, but one thing to look out for is whether it comes with separate crash and ride cymbals or one crash/ride. There's little point getting a kit without a ride as they'll need both crash and ride in no time at all and to buy a cymbal stand and ride at a later date ends up being quite expensive (relatively speaking). There's a couple of drum shops near me that sell quite a good Mapex starter kit that doesn't have separate ride and crash cymbals, but they do an upgrade to add a ride and stand at a reduced price. Of course if your pupil's budget can stretch a little further then kits such as the Yamaha Stage Custom and Pearl Vision can be considered which are great because they'll last them for years to come. In fact they'd only probably need to change drum kit if they're going pro (apart from maybe adding some shiny different cymbals or a good snare, which we all enjoy!).

With cheap electronic drums, again there's some rubbish out there (with pretty shoddy racks that don't hold up well after a while), so having a few ideas of decent electronic kits at some different price ranges is sensible too. Obviously electronic kits are an excellent option for people if noise and space are issues, as they can be for many students, but it's worth bearing in mind that electronic kits don't always hold their value as much as acoustic drums do.

I tend to encourage my students to go to a local drum shop rather than buying a kit online. They know more about what's available and suitable for different students with different budgets and needs than I do, and it's good to support them. It also means pupils get the chance to see and play what they're hoping to buy. I have a friend who has a deal with his local drum shop where they offer his pupils a small discount and they also give him a discount too as he's sent them business. Another thing you can do is when one of your students is selling their kit, presuming the kit's of reasonable quality, tell your other students as they can save money by getting a second-hand kit. It's worth remembering that sometimes new drum kits arrive boxed and in parts (no heads on), so some of your students might need a hand or bit of advice putting it together.

Skype Teaching

When I started writing this book, the only thing I wanted to write about but didn't have first hand experience of was Skype teaching. Rather than just going on the Internet to research it and basing this chapter on that, I wanted to make sure I actually knew something about what I was writing. I put up an ad on a drummers forum and arranged to give some Skype lessons to a few people. First and foremost, let me say it turned out to be far more fun and far better for teaching than I'd imagined. In actual fact I've now started doing some online teaching myself because of it (including continuing with some of the people I'd used as my guinea pigs!).

Skype teaching is growing quickly. It's great for us teachers as it means the pool of possible students has grown massively. Rather than just being able to teach students from your local area, you can now teach anyone who speaks your language from anywhere in the whole world, quite possibly without even leaving your house - game changer! There's also the added bonus that teaching people in different time zones gives. There's probably not that many students in your area wanting lessons on a weekday morning, but what's morning for you could be afternoon or evening in another country. This could help you be able to spread your lessons over the hours that are most suited to you. For students it's great because they don't have to travel anywhere and they can play on their own kit which they're comfortable with. If there are no good teachers in their local area, that's no longer a problem because they can choose a teacher from anywhere in the world!

If you're a teacher who has a particular specialism, or particularly enjoy teaching a certain level or age of pupil, then it's entirely possible that you could teach only that. For example, if you're really good at teaching double pedal, you can advertise yourself as the double pedal teacher. As I mentioned earlier, in your local area this might get you a few students, but when it comes to all the English speaking countries and people in the world, if you advertise properly, I dare say you could have a full teaching schedule doing just that. Similarly as a student, if you really wanted to go in-depth with your jazz playing you could find an online teacher who specialises in that instead of having to settle for a local teacher who plays a bit of jazz, but it's not their main thing.

Let's look first at the equipment you'll need. A computer with Skype on (I'd like to think this is rather obvious!), a webcam, some form of microphone and speakers, and a drum kit. Most laptops, iMacs etc have these built in anyway. You'll need to set it up so you can be clearly heard and most importantly so that your student can see you clearly at the kit for demonstrations. I've read of some people having a separate camera set up for their feet. If you're intending to do a lot of Skype teaching, multiple cameras could be worth considering, but are by no means a pre-requisite (at the time of writing I don't believe you can have multiple camera feeds showing on the screen at once, but you can switch between cameras).

What do your students need? Well, the same as you – Skype, a computer with microphone and speakers, and a camera. Their drum kit can be acoustic or electronic and I've taught one pupil on just a practice pad (it obviously narrows down what you can work on, but works fine). I'd also strongly suggest they have a metronome or click so you can hear them play rudiments etc. at certain tempos (it needs to be their end and not yours as there is a very slight time lag).

I'd strongly suggest giving a free introductory lesson to each student before starting online lessons. It only needs to be short, but you can talk about what they're hoping to achieve from the lessons and you can hear them play a bit. More importantly, you can use it to check the internet connection and make sure it's possible for their webcam to be set up for you to see their playing. It's vital that both of you have a pretty good internet connection otherwise the video link won't be very reliable. The video continually stopping or slowing down is no way to conduct a lesson, so use this first lesson to check that. Also it gives the student a chance to talk to you, see you and hear your suggestions as to what they need to improve and how you intend to go about this.

You're going to be asking for them to pay for their lessons up front (never give a Skype lesson before you've received payment as there's no other way to ensure you get paid by people who could live anywhere in the world, and you'll never meet face-to-face). Equally, this introductory lesson can help people trust you and be comfortable parting with their hard-earned cash. It might also be worth considering offering some sort of guarantee to students that if a lesson is severely interrupted due to technical issues then you'll make that lesson up at another time.

Preparation

Once you've got past the fact that you're not actually teaching someone in the same room as you (this doesn't take too long), then there's one main area that I think you need to consider with online teaching and that's preparation. You can't just hand your student a sheet of music or book to play from. Similarly you can't just say that you're going to play along to a certain tune in today's lesson and expect them to have that song on their computer/mp3 player (as you might have on yours). One Skype feature that's a massive help for online teaching is the ability to send files over it. While on your video call you can send pdfs, mp3s, documents etc. to your student using Skype. Almost equally excellent is the fact that if your student opens a document on their screen while on a video call with you, Skype automatically shows a little window at the top of the screen with the video feed of you in it. This means that your student can be playing from notated drum music (in pdf format) on their screen whilst still being able to see you. This function and the ability to send files are two of the things that helped make the Skype teaching work so well for me. Having really only used Skype to chat with family abroad before I'd never even considered these features.

However, you need to have spent time preparing beforehand to take advantage of these features. Basically, you need to turn all your teaching material into pdfs. Some stuff you might already have on your computer so it can easily be turned into pdfs (most programmes have an option to export documents as pdfs, if not then try downloading something like "pdf creator"). Other material you might need to scan (remember copyright still applies). I have a whole load of worksheets I've created in Sibelius that I use in my 'offline' teaching. I've turned every single one into a pdf, so now I can email them or send them to students over Skype as needed in a format that's easily read by anyone. If you've got any backing tracks you've created, you can send those over too as mp3s, otherwise you'll need to tell your students in advance and they can make sure they have the track on their computer before the lesson.

In offline lessons you'll write down what your student needs to practise, with online teaching I'd strongly advise using email for this. After each lesson send your student an email outlining what they need to practise. You can also include links to any relevant material you've discussed (a YouTube link of a particular track for example) and attach any other necessary files. If you haven't arranged another lesson already then you can do that in this email too. Similarly, if needed, before each lesson you can email over any relevant files and make sure they've got any necessary mp3s ready. If you ever need to transfer big files then I've found Dropbox really useful (*www.dropbox.com*). In fact if you're doing a lot of online teaching and there's certain material you find yourself using with most students, then you could always have a collection of files uploaded there that you can share in one go rather than sending each one individually in lessons.

Video Recording

One other helpful option that's available to you with online teaching is the ability to record the lesson, and not just the audio, the video too. As part of your service you could send students a video of each lesson (you can't email such large files, but something like Dropbox would work so you can upload and share). This would mean you'd have to record and upload the lesson yourself, or instead you could suggest your students install a programme and do this themselves. Alternatively, you could add "receive a video recording of each lesson" as a premium lesson option that's available if people want to pay extra for this. The obvious advantage of having a video of the lesson is that your students can refer to it later. If they've forgotten something you said or demonstrated, or just wish to go over something again, it's all there. It could also be a good way for the student to see their progress from the lesson itself to their current practice session. Let's be honest, for any musician, the ability to listen back to their playing can often be enlightening!

Obviously, depending on whether it's you or your student doing the recording, you'll need to check that the programme you use has the ability to record what you want. For example, if you're recording for your student then make sure the programme you choose allows you to record what THEY are seeing (the feed you are sending) and not just what is on your screen (them!). With some programmes you can record a video showing both feeds (often called side-by-side), this seems to be the best option to me. This way, not only can your student watch your demonstrations again, but also see the mistakes they made which you highlighted. This can be a lot easier to do when they watch the lesson back than it is for them to be aware of during the lesson when they're playing.

More programmes seem to exist for PC than Mac, but here's a selection of programmes that enable you to record Skype video. Have a look to find out which suits you best (some have a function that automatically uploads your videos to Dropbox, which could definitely save you time). Some of them are free and even the paid ones seem to offer free trials:

Supertintin
Evaer
Pamela
Callnote
Call recorder for Mac

You can find these and more in the "Call Recording (audio and video)" section in the Skype shop *Apps Directory*.

Pricing and Payments

It's important to get the price of your lessons right. First of all, look at other teachers in your area and find out how much they charge (it could be guitar or drum teachers). If you're going to be teaching online Skype lessons, again, do some research to see what others charge. Most countries' Musicians Unions usually have suggested lesson fees, so it's definitely worth finding out what they are. Hopefully these steps will help give you a ballpark figure of what to charge. Think about your prices for different lesson lengths like 30 minutes and 1 hour.

Whatever you decide to do, don't price yourself too low even if you're just starting out. It can be tempting to charge less than other teachers to attract students, but actually it's a bad idea. It can create the wrong impression to potential students and suggest that you're cheaper because you're not as good a teacher. People tend to be looking for the teacher they think is best or most suitable for them, not the cheapest.

If you're travelling to students' houses to teach then consider charging extra for these mobile lessons as you'll be incurring travel costs and it takes more of your time. People don't mind paying a little extra for convenience. As well as students paying for each lesson individually, you might want to consider selling blocks of lessons. For example, giving people the option of paying for a block of say 5 or 10 lessons in advance. This can make life easier for everyone. I know some teachers who offer a small discount if people pay in blocks, I personally don't, but it's something to consider. This is something you could do with Skype lessons too, but bear in mind people may not be comfortable doing this immediately. Students might not want to send 10 lessons worth of fees up front to you (as we've said, someone they'll probably never meet in the flesh) until they've had a few lessons and come to trust you - I know I wouldn't if it was the other way round!

Finally, it's worth considering increasing your fees a little every year or two. Inflation and the cost of living go up, so your prices need to as well.

Contracts

If you start doing a lot of teaching and particularly if you're working in schools, it can be a good idea to have contracts. The income is something you rely upon so you can't have people not turning up, not paying or stopping lessons at the drop of a hat. A contract can outline things like the amount of notice people need to give if they need to cancel a lesson (for example, 48 hours notice is needed or the lesson will be forfeited – i.e. they still have to pay for it). You could set a certain amount of weeks notice needed in order to stop lessons (4 weeks or something like that, this gives you a chance to find someone else to fill their slot). You could also outline how many lessons the student should expect over a certain period of time. For example 30 lessons a school year, or you could say how many per semester/term. Organisations like the Musicians Union have standard templates for teaching contracts that members can download. As well as giving you job security, it also shows potential students that you're serious and professional about your teaching business. If you're just starting out with a few students this isn't really necessary, but if teaching becomes a significant part of your income it's worth doing.

Payment Arrangements

You need to consider how to arrange being paid. There are several ways to choose from, it really is up to you. Are pupils going to pay cash at every lesson? This means they've always got to have cash and you've always got to have change (probably impractical if you're teaching lots of lessons). As discussed in the pricing section, you could also get people to pay for lessons in blocks, i.e. 5 or 10 at a time, this can be more practical. You can then be paid by cash, cheque or I imagine we'll gradually move to many more students paying by bank transfer (just make sure they clearly state their name in the payment details so you know who's paid!). Think about what suits you and your students best, you can always discuss with them how they'd like to pay when starting lessons. A mixture of people paying cash, cheque and bank transfer can be good (obviously payment options might be different from country to country, but you get the general principle). You get money in your bank account to pay bills and some cash to spend too.

For Skype lessons you could use bank transfer or invoice via PayPal. As mentioned earlier, I would strongly recommend being paid in advance for online teaching to make sure you're not taken advantage of. PayPal can be useful for people paying you from other countries, but take into account that they will take a small percentage for processing the payment, so factor this into your pricing.

Invoicing

When people are paying for blocks of lessons you might want to give them an invoice stating how much is to be paid, when by and how you can be paid (include your bank details). It's easy enough to bash up a quick template for these on the computer that you can use, or there are also some invoicing apps out there you could have a look at (including some good free ones). When people are paying you via PayPal, there's a "Request Money" section in your account where again you can make a template and just fill in the relevant details each time.

If you're teaching a lot of lessons, I recommend having a book (or spreadsheet) where you write down all your "INS" - money received, and "OUTS" - money spent (be it on teaching material, paying a music shop a small amount to rent a room or paying for petrol if travelling). This can help keep track of things when it comes to tax.

It's really important to keep a diary, that way you can keep track of who's having lessons when. When students pay for a block of lessons in advance you can also keep track of how many of these lessons they've received. For example you could mark down 7/10 if it's their 7th lesson of 10 paid for. That way you won't accidentally invoice students when they're still owed "paid for" lessons, and you won't give them extra free ones. Students sometimes forget how many they've had too, and this means you can tell them exactly how many lessons they've had of those paid for in advance and give them dates if needed. Again, it's all about professionalism and making your life easier.

Website Building

I t's obvious that if you're only going to be doing Skype teaching then you're going to need a website. You're not going to be getting local students, you're going to be advertising all over the world, so the only way people can learn about you and your teaching will be through your website and the internet. However in this day and age, I think every drum teacher should have a website whether teaching one-to-one lessons in your local area or doing Skype lessons, especially if you're just starting out or if you're trying to grow your business and get more students.

If you're trying to find out information about something, be it a hotel to stay in, an electrician or the best martial arts lessons locally, what do you do? Probably google it. We use the Internet to search for so much information these days and it's becoming more accessible via our laptops, tablets and phones. What is someone who's looking for a drum teacher going to do? If they happen to be lucky enough to have a friend who's having drum lessons they might ask them, but it's much more likely that they'll type "drum lessons (insert whatever area you live in!)" into a search engine and press enter. They'll have a list of possible local teachers in seconds. The sites at the top of this search in particular will get lots of traffic (people clicking and visiting their site), but more about that in the Search Engine Optimisation (SEO) section later.

Now you know you need a website (if you didn't already!), it's time to find out how to build one. It's pretty easy to do it yourself and costs practically nothing (from $18). I have musician friends who've had websites built for them professionally from £500 upwards and they look no better than ones I've built myself for the cost of a few beers (unless you live in Norway, then it's the price of a mouthful of beer!), and I started out just like most of you, with little or no experience. I did outsource the programming and design of my *www.brocksterdrums.com* site (through *www.odesk.com*) as I had a very specific look in mind, but even then it cost me less than a decent crash cymbal! Right now a few of you are thinking "I've done stuff like that before, shouldn't be a problem", some of you are thinking "Okay, I'll give it a go", and some of you are thinking "it's all very well for you to say, but I've never done anything like that before, there's no way I could do it". Well I'm going to help explain how, so read on and give it a go!

Let's briefly talk about choosing your website name. You want your domain name (web address that people type into their browser) to be your website name. There are a few things to consider when choosing. Do you want to go by your own personal name, create a unique business name or go for something that's good for search engines? For example *brocksterdrums.com*, *bangthatdrum.com* or *drumlessonscambridge.co.uk*. They've all got their advantages and disadvantages. *brocksterdrums.com* and *bangthatdrum.com* are probably more memorable than *drumlessonscambridge.co.uk*, but *drumlessonscambridge* is going to do well if someone searches for "drum lessons cambridge". If you think you're going to use your site for more than teaching, then perhaps your own name is wise (I've gone for *brocksterdrums.com,* which is based on my surname/nickname), then you can use it to show different areas of your drumming. If you want to give your teaching business a name (e.g. Bang that Drum) then go for *bangthatdrum.com* or *co.uk.* If you're thinking big, this could allow you to grow your business and employ other tutors in the future under the same established business name. If you're only going to use your site to advertise drum lessons and only want to teach locally, then *drumlessons_(placename)_* and *drumteacher_(placename)_* are strong candidates. You should also think about the TLD (top level domain), the extension bit at the end of your domain name. People often type *.com* by default, so if you're doing something like Skype teaching or going for a personal name website, I'd strongly advise that. If you're offering a local service though, you should use your country's TLD (for example *.co.uk* or *.de*) as it's more relevant for people doing local searches.

This brings me to the last point on website/domain names. Before you settle on a name for your business/website, just check the domain name, complete with the TLD you want, is available. Google "domain names" and loads of sites where you can check the availability of domain names will come up. If it's not available, then do seriously consider how important the name is to you as opposed to not having the TLD you want. It might be worth choosing a different name instead of losing traffic to a competitor with a similar name. Also it might mean there's already a business with the same name, another possible reason why you might want to change your initial name idea or at least alter it slightly. For example, when I started writing this book, pretty much from day one it had the working title "How to Teach Drums". As I continued writing, I thought I wanted to stick with that name as the title, but found that *howtoteachdrums.com* was rudely already owned by someone else! So I had to decide whether I wanted to go for something like *howtoteachdrums.net* or *.co.uk*, change the book's title altogether, or try something else more subtle. I weighed up all the options, and decided to go with the minor change to *www.how2teachdrums.com*. The title and the *.com* are both important to me and having '2' instead of 'to' isn't uncommon in web addresses. I happen to think the 2 might make it more memorable, but I figured more people are likely to find my book in a Google search than by directly typing in the address anyway. That's my choice, for my reasons and only time will tell if I was right. If you can't get exactly the domain name you want first off, weigh up the different options and think about what's most suitable for you.

Content

Before you start trying to create your website, have a think about what pages you want and some of the wording, videos etc. you want to include. You want your homepage to outline briefly who you are and what you do as well as being rich in keywords for SEO (more about this later). What other pages you choose to have is up to you, but think about what you'd want to know if you were thinking of having lessons with someone. Also, look at other teachers' websites to see what you think works (and what doesn't!). Some of these might be good: Biography/About, Teaching, Lesson Videos, Online Lessons, Rates/Prices, Links. Whatever pages you choose to add, you must have a contact page, and don't just write down your email address, add a contact form (easy to do this with Wordpress). I've found that more people contact me via my website using the contact form than email. Maybe it's because people are lazy and it means they've only got to fill in the boxes in the form as opposed to writing an email, for whatever reason, it seems to work. Once you've been teaching for a little while it would be great to add a testimonials page with a few complimentary comments from your students. That way it's not just you saying you're good, somebody looking for a drum teacher can take the word of some of your students too.

Another section some teachers have on their websites is a special login area for students. It could give them exclusive access to lesson pdfs, click tracks, backing tracks and any other material you choose. It's another added extra for your teaching and could be used equally for offline and online students.

Wordpress.com

So you've decided on your domain name and have some idea of the content you want. Now it's time to create your website. There are hundreds of sites that let you create websites for free, so have a look around and see what's out there. I'm going to give you a few details about how I've easily and cheaply created websites that look good. We're going to be using *www.wordpress.com* (it's really popular because it's straightforward, good for SEO and there's a very active forum should you need help). If you want more customisation, widgets and features, and have some experience with website building already then you should definitely consider using *wordpress.org*. The final result will probably be better, but it's not as straightforward (although still relatively uncomplicated) and you'll also need to pay for some hosting. Designing your actual website is a similar process whether you go for *wordpress.com* or *.org*, but for now we'll concentrate on *wordpress.com*.

You might know Wordpress as a blogging site, which it is, but you can also create pages and add content easily without the need to know anything about html or coding. You just type in the words you want, add links to any videos etc. and it automatically turns this into html, and therefore a webpage for you - perfect!

First you need to sign up to *wordpress.com,* which is completely free. You'll initially choose your blog URL at sign up (_____.*wordpress.com*), you should make this the name you want your website to be called, but don't worry, you can get rid of the 'wordpress.com' bit in the address later - that's what you pay the same as a few beers for, but you might as well make sure you're happy with what you've created first.
Wordpress.com has a support section where there are a number of tutorials on getting started, customising your site, creating content, adding domains etc. that can be helpful and are well worth a read. I've

also written this short guide that should help with a few things too. Things change all the time in the cyber world we live in, but here's how you do it currently. Once logged in you can do everything you need from your Wordpress 'dashboard'.

You'll probably want to be able to play around with the look and content of your site without the world watching, so in the *Reading* area of the Settings menu choose the option that makes your website private. Just make sure you don't forget to change this once you're ready to unleash your efforts on the world or else you might find yourself wondering why no-one's visiting your site!

Next we need to make sure that any pages you create look like webpages and not blog entries. Go to the *Discussion* area of the Settings menu and uncheck "Allow people to post comments on new articles". When you create each page, at the bottom of the editing page there's a *Likes and Shares* section, you want to uncheck both "show likes" and "show sharing buttons". These few steps should get rid of all the blog like bits on your pages. If there are any other bits that turn up on your page to do with sharing, comments, likes etc. then have a search around the dashboard. There's usually some way to get rid of them.

Next up it's time to create your pages (*Add New* in the Pages section), you can add more content later, but initially just create the pages you're going to want and add a few words on each page. Make sure you're using the "Visual" tab not the "Text" tab to edit your page (it normally automatically goes to Visual anyway), you can see this in the top right hand corner of the box you're writing your text content in. You'll need to publish each page, but don't worry, remember no-one else can see them yet. This allows you to get your page menu up and running and also gives you a chance to play around with your site's appearance. Call the page you want to be your homepage "Home" for now (although it's unlikely you'll want to change that).

Now go to the *Menus* area of the Appearance section. Create a menu and give it any name you like! Drag your pages around in the menu structure area into the order you want them to be in, and save. In the menu settings area below, select the "Primary Navigation" option to tell your site to use this menu.

You now need to make "Home" your homepage by going to *Reading* in the Settings menu, otherwise it won't show a static homepage, it'll instead want to show your latest blog entry. In *Front Page Displays* choose "A Static Page" and then select "Home" in the Front page option. After following these options you'll now have a homepage that's automatically displayed when someone visits your site and your other pages will be listed in a menu structure making it easy for people to find the other sections of your site.

The next step is making your site look good. Firstly you need to choose a theme (*Themes* in the Appearance section). There are plenty of free ones and you can preview how they're going to look. Think about how you want your pages laid out. I'd consider having a main content area with a sidebar. Often to the right of the page this sidebar will allow you to have an area to add Twitter feeds, a Facebook Like Box, some static text etc. This area will stay the same for all your pages with just the main content area changing (although you can usually change the sidebar to only display on certain pages if needed). Choose the theme you want and activate it. If you're not sure, go for something simple and clean looking. You want something that looks professional where people can easily read the content and not be distracted. There are quite a few homemade websites out there that just look rubbish and amateurish. As soon as you load them, regardless of the quality of any content, they've already given you the wrong impression. That's why we're using Wordpress, your site's not going to be one of them!

Once you've chosen your theme you can then customize it using the other menus in the Appearance section. Different themes have different things you can customize so have a look around at what the options are for your theme. You can sometimes change colour options and also this is where you do the important bit of creating a header for your site. This header appears at the top of all your pages and will give your site its personal look, so it's important to get it right. You can upload a relevant photo here if you have one (likely to include some drums!) or if you're not happy with what you have you might want to consider outsourcing and getting someone to create one for you (using something like odesk.com you can outsource your header for a price you set in dollars). You can get this done for much less than you'd think and it will help your site stand out from the crowd. If you're any good in photoshop you could try creating one yourself, it says in the header section what size in pixels you need to make it. You can also customize things like your site title and tagline – use the tagline as a few word description of your site.

Adding widgets can also be done in the Appearance section. Widgets add features and content to your sidebar. You'll see there are numerous widgets here you can drag into the "Primary Widget Area" on the right that will then appear in your site's sidebar. You can also remove widgets you don't want from here too (recent posts, archives, categories etc. that are blog-related and often put in the sidebar area by default). The Twitter widget would be a good one to add as would the Facebook Like Box (this can only be used for Facebook pages not ordinary profiles, don't underestimate the difference). You could also add a text area if you wanted something appearing on all of your pages (special offers or a specific testimonial, have a think). Basically, this is the time when you generally play around and make your site look good. Have a look at all the different options and see what you can do.

Once that's done it's time to start editing the pages you've created to flesh out the content (there's a preview option so you can see how things would look when published). If you want to add any YouTube videos to your pages at all (a good idea to help show off your skills and stand out from other faceless websites), then it's really easy. Find the video's embed code on YouTube (usually in the sharing section found below the video), cut and paste this into your wordpress page and the video will show up when you publish the page. Adding photos is easy too, just click the "add media" button just above the main page editing area and upload your pictures. One thing to note is that you can't upload mp3s to a free wordpress.com page (you can if you're doing it using wordpress.org because then you've paid for separate hosting), but you can however link to mp3s and audio files if they're hosted somewhere else.

Once you've finished your site don't forget to go back to the *Reading* area and select "Allow search engines to index this site". This will make your site public and allow search engines to find it. I'd suggest getting a couple of mates to have a look at it in case you've made any glaring mistakes. When you're happy, it's time to spend those few quid and buy the domain name (which of course you've already checked is available....). Go to the *Store* area and choose "Add a Domain". Here you can buy the domain name you want and then when people type *"whateveryouhavedecidedtocallyoursite.com"* they'll now go directly to your page.

Don't worry if you get stuck at any point, just search the *wordpress.com* forum as someone's probably already had the same problem and the answer may well be there. If you chose the *wordpress.com* option but found creating the site quite easy and want more customisation, you can always create a *wordpress.org* site to use instead. If you're going to make this change I'd say it's probably easier to do this before buying your domain name, because then you can buy your domain name and hosting together which will make your life easier. Happy website building!

SEO

SEO stands for Search Engine Optimisation. Basically it's all about getting your website to appear as high as possible in the list of results you see in search engines, so this section could also be called "How to get to the top of Google". A recent study showed that 53% of people clicked on the top search result of Google's organic listings (the unpaid results, so not the 2 or 3 paid for listings that appear at the very top), 15% on the second and 9% on the third. This just shows how important it is to get your website listed as high as possible. There are hundreds of books and blog articles about SEO you can read if you want to look into it further, but here's how to get started. I'm going to talk about Google as it's the most popular search engine, but these steps will help your website's ranking on all search engines. In short, what you want to do is make your website appear authoritative and relevant for your chosen keywords. There are two main areas to consider, these are called "on-page optimisation" and "off-page optimisation".

First let's talk about on-page optimisation. This is about the things you can do on your website itself to improve it's ranking. Initially what you need to do is choose your keywords. These are basically the words you think people will search for to find your service. Depending on exactly what sort of teaching you'll be doing and where, this could be things like "Drum Teacher Sydney" or "Drum Lessons Auckland". I can tell you for example that "Drum Lessons London" gets four times more searches than "Drum Teacher London" so picking the right keywords here could get you four times as much traffic! However, it's possible that "Drum Lessons London" might be more competitive as far as getting to the top of the search rankings goes. And don't even think about choosing

"Skype Drum Lessons". That gets 91 global searches per month, while "online drum lessons" gets 4400. It's a no brainer! I'd never have imagined the difference would be so astonishingly huge.

Choosing the wrong keywords to focus on there could literally be the difference between a successful business and failure. Google have a keyword tool that gives you these figures, so it's definitely worth finding out what people are searching for (just search for "Google keyword tool" and you'll find it).

Once you've decided on the keywords you want to focus on you need to get these featuring a fair bit in your homepage text. This is so that when somebody searches for "Drum Lessons New York", Google can see that your page is relevant because that term's mentioned a few times on your page. If you don't mention it, how on earth are Google's little robots supposed to know that this is what your site's about? Don't go over the top though, you want to make your site readable and natural to the people who find it (and also Google may well penalize you if you use the keywords a silly amount of times).

If you're using *wordpress.com* to create your website, then you definitely want your keywords to feature in your sites tagline (find it in *General* in the Settings menu). Then also include the keywords in your page's text a few times (especially once very near the beginning). You can have different pages of your site focusing on different keywords. So you might choose "online drum lessons" for your homepage's keywords, but there's no reason why if you wanted to concentrate on jazz teaching you couldn't use "jazz drum lessons" as your keywords on one of your sites other pages. If you've chosen to use *wordpress.org* then there are plugins such as Yoast that help with SEO.

Whereas on-page optimisation is about things you can do on your website to show Google that your page is relevant to certain keyword searches, off-page optimisation is about other things on the internet (aside from your site) that show Google your page is authoritative. For off-page optimisation it's all about getting good quality links to your page. If Google sees quite a few other websites linking to yours, then it thinks your website must be ok! Don't just go for links on any old rubbish sites though, that can harm you. Make sure the links are on a mixture of well regarded and relevant websites, otherwise Google will think they're only there to help your search ranking (which of course they are, but by placing the links on appropriate sites, it's not too obvious!) . If it's a site where you can include your keywords in the description that page has of your website/service as well as your web address, then that helps too. Look for relevant directories for drum teachers and also general music stuff in your area to add your details to. Putting up ads on gumtree/craigslist etc. will also help simply because you're getting your web address in more, relevant places (and having the added bonus of making it visible to potential students at the same time). Having a YouTube channel that links to your site as well as a Facebook page and Twitter account is good too.

As I've said, there's lots of info you can read about SEO and we've barely scratched the surface, but basically it's about choosing good keywords, featuring them in the text of your pages and then getting good quality links to your site from other websites.

YouTube Videos

YouTube videos can be helpful for a few reasons. They'll help promote you to possible customers (both local people who find you via the Internet and for Skype lessons) and can help with Google rank and generally getting more traffic to your website. If you do them well they make you look professional and they can also be used not only to show your drumming skills, but more importantly your new found teaching skills.

Think about who your "ideal customers" are and what they want to learn. If your ideal customer is a rock drummer, then a video of you playing a jazz tune isn't the best idea, maybe a Led Zepp track or something by the Foo Fighters might be better (work out the sort of bands they'll be into). Then they can watch your video and think, "Hey, he/she's cool and I want to be able to play that song like them". Doing a brief lesson could be a great idea and make you stand out from the crowd. You could explain how to play a basic beat or even better, choose a beat from a song your ideal customer might be into and teach that beat by breaking it down and playing it slower etc. This shows that not only can you play, but you can teach too.

So, how do you make this video? Chances are you've already got everything you need without realising it. You've probably got either iMovie or Windows Movie Maker on your computer (if you really get into making videos you might want to look into upgrading to something like Final Cut or Sony Vegas). If you've got a digital camcorder already, great, but most people don't. Most digital cameras have a pretty good video function, but failing that, use your phone (or borrow a mate's camera).

If you're lucky enough to have mics and an audio interface to record your drums, great, but the audio from your camera will do for now. You're not using the videos to sell your sound, it's about showing your playing and teaching skills. If it turns out the inbuilt mic on your camera's rubbish (sometimes they're a bit tinny or don't like the high volume of the drums), then you could always do your video lesson on a practice pad to get round this. Some of the portable mp3 recorders are quite cheap and record pretty good sound (Zoom do one which also does video, well worth considering).

Tidy the area around your kit and then work out what you want to play/teach. If you're going to do any talking, decide an outline of what you're going to say before you press record. If you'd rather not talk, you can easily add on screen text in the video instead. Talking might make it a bit more personal though and the prospective student might get the chance to feel they connect with you a bit more.

Once recorded, upload the video to your computer and import it into iMovie or Windows Movie Maker. Add any text you might want over the video and also a few words at the beginning and end (keep it short though, you don't want people changing to someone else's video!), just your web address and name of the video would do. Use your programme to render this all into a video and upload it to YouTube (set up a YouTube channel with a suitable name, for example I use *youtube.com/BrocksterDrums* for my general drumming and teaching related videos, and *youtube.com/onlinesessiondrums* for my online session drumming). If you're trying to get work in your local area for example, you could go for DrumLessonsCambridge, or you could use your website name or personal name.

Only now do we get to the really important stuff, making sure people actually find and watch your video! Writing the title, description and tags for your video and including the right keywords is vital. In the title make sure you put what the video's about "How to play a Rock drum beat", "Learn Black in Black by Drum Teacher Oxford" or "Online Drum Lessons: When the Levee Breaks".

In the description, write a few words about the video's content, but also make sure to say "if you're looking for drum lessons in the Cambridge area visit www.DrumLessonsCambridge.com". If you have sheet music for the video lesson then you could include a link to the pdf.

In the tags, put not only things like "drum lessons" "learn drums" "drum teacher" and what the lesson's about "rock beat" "rock drums" "music", but add your area "Liverpool" too. If you're going to do Skype lessons then include something like "online drum lessons" and "Skype lessons" - you get the picture. Basically, think about all the possible things somebody looking for your services might type into Google/YouTube if searching for lessons, and then get those words into your title, description and tags somewhere.

You've now got a product to show potential pupils not only who you are and what you do, but another possible way of them finding out about you. How many of the local drum teachers in your area have this? Probably not that many.

Advertising

dvertising is a vital part of your business. There's no point having good ideas about what to teach and how to teach it, as well as a good looking website and videos if no-one knows about you and has no way of finding out about you. You might as well not bother. It's not particularly difficult though and can be really fun and worthwhile. It's something a lot of drum teachers aren't great at, so a bit of time and effort on your part should really help put you ahead of the competition. If you're teaching in your local area then I'd recommend using a mixture of both offline and online advertising, whereas for Skype teaching it's likely to be mostly online.

Offline Advertising

Offline advertising doesn't have to cost much, if anything at all. You can advertise in magazines, but often that can be expensive and no more effective than free advertising so I'd suggest trying the other suggestions here before you give that any real thought. Get yourself some business cards made up (there are plenty of sites like Vistaprint where you can do it cheaply). Then not only can you give these to individuals but you can also pin your business card to noticeboards too. Places like local shops, rehearsal studios, music shops, and the post office are good for this - anywhere where people are standing in a queue getting bored (a perfect captive audience who are looking for any distraction and will be delighted to think about drum lessons instead)!

You could have an ad put up in the Music Department of local schools (maybe send a few flyers to the Head of Music/Music co-ordinator). Local free ads and classifieds are also worth considering. There are doubtless plenty of other cunning places I haven't thought of, so have a think.

This one might seem obvious, but don't forget to tell people that you're available for drum lessons. Tell your friends, other musicians, your Mum, anyone. You don't need to be in their faces, but just mentioning it to them can't hurt. That way when they hear someone saying "my child/friend is thinking of playing drums" they can suggest you as a teacher. Word of mouth is a great thing, particularly when you've got a few students and they start suggesting you to their friends.

Online Advertising

There are literally hundreds of places you can advertise for free online, but try to spend your time wisely by thinking about where the people you want to teach are likely to look/hang out online. Gumtree, Craigslist, Kijiji etc. are usually good places as are local community sites and local and national musicians sites. Most sites have an appropriate forum, classifieds or directory section. There are also a number of music teacher websites that often have lists of teachers so get yourself added to those too. A good side product of these ads is that the more places your web address appears online, on relevant pages, the more it'll help with SEO.

If you wanting to offer Skype teaching, then the only place people are likely to find you is online so get a Facebook page and Twitter account (it's worth thinking outside the box though, there might be some worthwhile offline places to advertise if you give it some thought). As mentioned already a YouTube channel with some good videos is a must too, this is a really great way of people finding out about you. If they love your drumming and see that they can get Skype lessons from you, then that's great free advertising, and half your work is done as they already like your playing and want to learn from you specifically. Be active on Twitter and your Facebook page by giving teaching tips and links and you can also direct people to your video lessons from there. Make sure it's not all about you and selling though. People see right through it. Get a good balance of teaching comments, things advertising you and your service and general drumming stuff. Don't be bland, try to put a bit of personality into it as people will feel like they're getting to know you and are more likely to follow you.

You might want to consider paying to run Google ads too (called adwords). I'd be wary of spending too much on these though as whilst they might get traffic to your website, there's no guarantee you'll get work from these extra visitors. Certain, more popular keywords can be expensive so I'd recommend looking around as there are usually free Google adwords vouchers to be had.

Ad Writing

Again a little thought here can really be worth it. What's going to make people contact you over other drummers whose adverts they see? I'd suggest making your ads and possibly even your business cards too, quite specific/targeted. Anyone can write "all ages, all styles, all abilities", it's not really going to make you stand out from the crowd and relate directly to the person reading it (maybe you do teach all styles, all ages and all abilities but you need to focus your ads).

Is there a certain area you specialize in? Is there a certain group that's not being catered for in your area or in online Skype lessons? For example, you could say you specialize in Rock and teaching adults. It's targeted, but still quite a large group. If an adult who wants drum lessons reads it, they think "rock, yeah, that's exactly what I want to learn and this teacher specializes in teaching people just like me, I'll give them a call". Mr "all styles/all ages" ad is going to be much less appealing than yours to this person. Or you could point out that you specialize in teaching beginners. Quite a lot of people looking for drum lessons are beginners so you're pointing out something you focus on while still appealing to a wide audience. You (specialized teacher) 1 - Mr all styles, all abilities (dull) 0! I'd recommend playing around with different ads (particularly on gumtree etc), if one doesn't work, try something different next time.

How to Keep Work

You've got all your shiny, eager new students due to advertising in the right way and in the right places, you know what you want to teach them, but how do you keep hold of them? Well for the most part it's quite simple, be reliable and on time. It's the same for gigs, but it never ceases to amaze me how bad some people are at it. I've had several students in the past who've left their previous drum teacher and started learning with me because their old teacher was unreliable. They may have had good material or been potentially a good teacher, I've no idea and it makes no difference, because they've lost a student and I've gained one.

If your lesson's arranged for 5.30pm, don't regularly turn up at 5.40pm, it makes you look unprofessional, in fact scrub that, it IS unprofessional. Don't regularly cancel lessons, especially not at the last minute. Yes, we all need to cancel/re-arrange from time to time, but always try to give as much notice as possible. This applies equally for Skype lessons too. It's often these simple things that have nothing to do with your actual teaching ability that make a big difference, so don't underestimate their importance.

There are also things you can do with your teaching that will help keep students. Try to make your lessons enjoyable, I mean it's playing drums, so it's pretty fun anyway, but the way you cover material and the manner you teach it in makes a big difference. Obviously the quality of what you're teaching will count as well. If you're producing good, well-rounded drummers, then they'll want to stay with you, someone they trust and respect. Do spend time on your *Drumming Timeline* making sure you've got a good idea of what you want to teach your pupils in order for them to continually improve and progress. Listen to your pupils and what they tell you they want to gain from lessons when they start with you. If they've already been playing for a while but have come to you specifically to improve say their left foot independence and reading skills, then make sure you take that into account and spend time working on those things (probably alongside other material you think will help them improve generally, but don't forget their specific goals and reasons for coming to you in the first place).

Finally, I've found that the pupils who stop lessons are often the ones that don't practise (however much you encourage them to). They tend to progress slowly and you're always covering the same material in lessons, which can get a bit tedious (for both of you), so encourage them to play/practise as much as possible outside of lessons. Sadly however much you try, there'll always be some people who just don't bother.

Hopefully you'll keep lots of your students for many years, but if not don't fret (as long as you're doing the above), just put up some more adverts. Even better, if things really take off, start someone from your waiting list!

Bits and Bobs

You should now have a good idea of what you want to teach, how, where and how to advertise in order to get yourself students. You're pretty much ready to go out there and put it all into practise. Finally I just want to touch briefly on a few other areas I think might be relevant to you as you start teaching.

What to Wear

I'll only write a little bit about what to wear when teaching, but it's definitely worth mentioning and it comes back to professionalism again. As drummers we can usually slouch about in whatever clothes we want (although sometimes we have to wear specific clothes or dress in a certain style for gigs - the less said about what I had to wear to play for Robyn at the BBC Big Weekend Festival the better!). This is not always possible when teaching though. I'm not saying don't be yourself, far from it, we're drummers and that's why people are employing us to teach drums. If you're teaching privately (i.e. not in a school), just make sure you're not looking too scruffy and at least have showered in the last couple of days! It's just a case of coming across in a fashion that shows you're serious about your teaching (especially to parents of school age students) rather than some long haired, scruffy drummer who drinks JD every night until 2am, has swear words on their T-shirt and isn't too bothered about teaching (OK so I overdid it a bit, but you get the idea). When teaching in schools I've generally found I'm expected to wear similar clothes to the normal teaching staff. In England that normally means smart. I can't say it's my favourite attire, I'm usually a jeans and T-shirt sort of girl, but there you are. While this all might seem obvious to some, it is worth having a quick think about.

Graded Exams

In some countries (particularly the UK, but in others like Australia and Canada too) it is possible to take Graded Exams in Drum Kit (and often Orchestral Percussion). If you live in a country where these are common, then I'd definitely suggest using them with some of your students.

Different exam boards have different syllabuses but for the most part the exam will involve your student preparing 2 or 3 set pieces along with some technical work (often rudiment based). It is common for at least one of these pieces to have a backing track accompaniment. There can also be other elements such as sight reading or quick study, aural and improvisation. Graded exams aren't right for every student but I find many respond well to them as it gives them something to work towards and a sense of achievement when they pass and receive a certificate. It can also be a good benchmark for the student to know what level they're at and gauge their progression. Aside from the motivation they can give your students, the very nature of the various elements needed to prepare for the exam can help to improve your students' reading, rudiments, playing to backing tracks, knowledge of styles and aural skills. If I have pupils studying music at school then they often use these exam pieces as part of the performance element of their school's exams.

Some students choose to learn the pieces but not take the exam. Other students just don't like the idea of exams and I'll never force them as it's counterproductive. If a pupil has specific learning difficulties they can sometimes find certain parts of the exam a struggle, but this is by no means always the case. If you contact the exam board, they'll often be able to give these pupils extra time and help in certain sections of the exam.

If you live in a country like the UK where drum kit exams are common and there are several different exam boards offering them, then I'd strongly advise you to have a look at them all. Being familiar with what's on offer from all the exam boards can help you choose the exams that suit your teaching best. Also, sometimes different exam boards are appropriate for different students. Each board will have their own approach. Some require you to memorize rudiments and others have studies where the rudiments are incorporated into a piece. Some have a wider diversity of styles included in their set pieces, while others are more Rock based. Recently in the UK Trinity Rock and Pop have released an exam syllabus where students learn actual songs by bands like Cream, Elbow and Green Day amongst others.

Here's a list of some exam boards based in the UK offering drum kit exams:

TrinityGuildhall: *www.trinitycollege.co.uk*
Trinity Rock and Pop: *trinityrock.trinitycollege.co.uk*
Rockschool: *www.rockschool.co.uk*
London College of Music: *www.uwl.ac.uk/lcmexams*

Orchestral Percussion

If the room you're teaching in has any Orchestral Percussion in it (this is probably more likely in a school) and you know how to play it, then it can be a great thing to teach your pupils. My students learn to play the snare drum as part of their drum kit work anyway. Notation reading, learning buzz rolls and playing duets on the snare are part and parcel of teaching drum kit for me. I know some teachers who start all their pupils on just the snare drum until they reach a certain level and only then will they let students progress onto drum kit. It's not the way I choose to go, I like to integrate things and teach both at the same time (once you've learnt to read and play a certain rhythm on the snare then apply it to the kit somehow, be it in a beat or fill), but it does ensure that pupils have a really solid grounding in technique and reading before they start playing the kit.

I find that introducing Timpani is something that students often enjoy due to their big, deep sound. Pupils can already read the rhythms from their snare playing so they often get the hang of it quite quickly. If your students have played piano before then Tuned Percussion is also worth introducing (if you play it yourself!). Their knowledge of the keyboard put together with their drumming technique really gives them a head start. If you don't play Orchestral Percussion or don't have access to the instruments, don't worry, but if you do, it's great to give your students as many Percussion skills as possible. It can also give school age pupils more opportunity of being able to play in various school ensembles.

Moeller Technique

Moeller technique is named after Sanford Moeller, who observed American Civil War drummers using the technique. His student Jim Chapin was a leading exponent of it in the second half of the twentieth century. You can use Moeller to play for long periods without injury or fatigue and amongst other things, it's great for accents.

I use a Moeller-like technique (I can't claim it to be pure Moeller, it's not, but it works for me!) almost all the time and it's great for so many reasons. Don't get me wrong, if you're a bad drummer, you'll be a bad drummer whether you know Moeller or not. There are plenty of excellent drummers who don't use Moeller, but it's a great thing to have some understanding of. It can allow good/advanced drummers to do things in a more economical way motion-wise and is especially helpful for accents and for grooves using one-handed 16th notes on the hi-hat.

It seems to me that Moeller has almost become a drumming holy grail to some and has some sort of reverence/mystery to it. There's no mystery, you just can't explain it adequately by writing it down, or dare I say by video alone (although the Jim Chapin Moeller DVD goes a very long way). It takes time and a very good teacher who really understands the mechanics of Moeller motion and this is one of the reasons I'm including this section. If you know/use Moeller technique then I personally would advise you to think very carefully about teaching it. Do you really understand the concept/mechanics completely and how to teach it? If yes then great, go ahead it'll be a wonderful thing to have in your teaching arsenal. If not, then consider steering clear or perhaps approaching it in a different way.

If you want to apply a Moeller-like motion on the hi-hats for your students (either for accent patterns or one handed 16th notes) then go for it, the principles will surely help them, but make sure they know you're just touching the tip of the iceberg and just because they're using that doesn't mean they "know Moeller technique". Instead you're just using its' principles to help you with a specific area. To be honest this is the most common use for a Moeller type technique in my teaching, but as I say I always point out we're just scratching the surface and are doing something based on Moeller technique as opposed to wrongly giving students the impression they've now mastered Moeller.

Hearing Protection

At the time of writing, I'm 34. I've had tinnitus since the age of 22 and I can assure you it's not all that fun. I've learnt to live with it, but have to be seriously careful. There's a high-pitched whistling noise and electrical buzzing type sound in my ears all the time. In the day I don't always notice it when there's background noise. At night I can hear it all the time and believe me, you don't want it. Other drumming related problems include hearing loss and I also read recently about a drummer who developed acute hyperacusis. This makes even normal volume, everyday sounds and noises painful to their ears and difficult to tolerate. It was as a direct result of their drumming and ended their playing career.

Fortunately it seems to me that drummers are becoming gradually more aware of hearing issues and are starting to think more about their ears. Don't think "Oh I'm young, I'll be fine" or, "I'll do something about that at some point". That's no good, you never know when it'll become a problem and by then it'll be too late.

Often as drum teachers we find ourselves teaching in small-ish spaces (I've refused to teach in rooms I think are really too small) for long periods of time. When you start teaching you'll find yourself exposed to more noise, for longer periods than before. I can't stress enough the fact that you should wear earplugs for ALL the drumming you do whether it's teaching, practising, gigging or even going to gigs. I've got some expensive moulded earplugs I use for gigging, but for teaching there are plenty of cheap earplugs available in music shops that'll do the trick. If you want to make a living out of the drums then it's really not optional, you must wear them. Your ears are too important to you. It's also worth discussing this with pupils and encouraging them to think about their hearing and get into good habits early.

Just one thing to note. When I first tried using earplugs it did take me a few weeks to get used to them, but I had no choice but to persist because of my tinnitus. Don't give up after one go. Use them while you're practising for a few weeks, then after a short time you'll feel comfortable enough to gig with them. You'll get so used to them that it feels weird without them, and your ears will thank you.

Helpful websites:

www.tinnitus.org.uk (British Tinnitus Association)
www.ata.org (American Tinnitus Association)
www.hearnet.com (Hearing education and awareness for Rockers!)

Child Protection

This is a really important issue for both you and your students. Instead of writing too much about it myself I'd rather guide you to organisations which can give you far better advice than I. If you're a member of a Union then they'll have some great information regarding teaching and Child Protection. For example:

American Federation of Musicians: ***http://www.afm.org***
Musicians Union (UK): ***http://www.musiciansunion.org.uk***

For the sake of your students and/or their parents it can be good if you have certain checks to show you don't have a criminal record. In the UK these are known as CRB checks (they've just changed their name to DBS "Disclosure and Barring Service" checks). Different countries have their equivalents to these and they can make parents of younger children especially, feel confident about you being alone with their child.

For your own sake, I'd advise wherever possible to teach in a room with some glass in the door or a window. If that's not possible then try to leave the door of the room you're teaching in slightly open. Sadly there are some people in this world who act improperly towards children, so by taking these steps you can help to cover yourself against any possible accusations.

Tax

As a drum teacher, you're likely to be self-employed. If you're doing a fair bit of teaching, have a website and are putting up adverts etc. then that makes you visible to the Taxman. Every country has a different system but rest assured they all involve you paying money somehow!

Keep records of all the money coming in (payments to you) and all that's going out that relates to your teaching (for example: travel, drumsticks, drum books and any money you might pay for the use of a teaching room). Make sure you keep notes regularly and keep all receipts etc. This counts equally for all your music based earnings. I do this in a cash book (you can get them in most stationary stores), but there's also plenty of software to help you with this. If you're going to be earning a full time living from music/teaching you might want to consider getting an accountant at some point.

Do be sure to put money aside towards your tax bill too (preferably on a regular basis). You could have a separate account and put a certain percentage of your income in there. I know too many musicians who have had a nasty shock come tax bill time when they haven't put enough aside and have to find the money from somewhere....

A couple of handy government websites:

http://www.irs.gov (Tax in the U.S.)
http://www.hmrc.gov.uk (Tax in the UK)

Public Liability

In the world we live in it's worth having Public Liability Insurance (again, some musicians' unions provide this).

In the extremely unlikely situation that someone injures themselves in your lesson (probably something larger than a splinter from a drumstick!) then you want to make sure you're covered. Public Liability Insurance generally isn't too expensive and depending on the policy will cover you against injury to members of the public, damage to property and any related legal fees. Some policies will cover you for your other musical activities too.

If you do get Public Liability Insurance then be sure to mention it on your website, as this again can help to create a good, professional impression of you and your teaching.

Conclusion

As a drummer looking to teach, whether full time or part time to help you diversify, having read this book you should be feeling more confident and equipped to go out and start teaching successfully.

You should now feel able to decide for yourself what to teach and how to go about it. By creating your own *Drumming Timeline,* listing in order all the things you think a student should learn, you're setting up your own curriculum and have a path your students can follow in order for them to progress. It also means much of your lesson planning is taken care of (don't get lazy though, there's always other things that crop up to work on and songs your students want to learn; mixing it up a little can make it more interesting for you too). Teach your students to read, get them playing to music as often as possible and encourage them to practise regularly. Remember, if they're struggling to play something then breaking things into sections and slowing them down are good places to start and will help much of the time. Encouraging your students will build their confidence and help them reach their potential.

Don't be tempted to take shortcuts with your teaching. By not spoon-feeding your students and helping them to work things out for themselves you're making them more independent. Be sure to give your students a good, thorough base of knowledge. Solid technique, reading ability, a sense of pulse and good ears will really help with a student's future progress. Yes, it might mean some of their early progress appears a little slower whilst covering these different areas, rather than just showing them how to play a rock beat and the dreaded 4 notes on each drum going round the toms fill. But it'll make both your and their lives a lot smoother in the long run. Of course, I'm not saying don't show them a basic rock beat near the beginning to give them a sense of achievement and something to play to their friends, far from it. This is one of the things they'll end up playing continuously for most of their drumming lives, I'm just saying do it as part of a wider set of ideas and skills.

Having decided what to teach and how to teach it you should now also have an idea of a number of places you could potentially teach at. Specific, targeted advertising both off and online should help you attract new students. Create a website for yourself and consider using social media too (especially for Skype teaching). Choosing the right keywords and optimising your site for them will help get traffic and make you visible to pupils searching for drum lessons.

The growing interest in Skype lessons also has such potential for us as teachers. It's only just beginning to take off, so if you can get in there early with a good website and advertising, you can put yourself in a great position as an established teacher with good testimonials as this area grows. Just make sure you've done the necessary preparation of having all your files in a format you can send to students. The added benefit of video recording can be such a good selling point. Online teaching also offers the real possibility of being able to specialise in teaching what you most enjoy and are strong at as you'll have so many more prospective students across the world. Some people might not even be aware that this type of teaching even exists so advertise as widely as possible. If you're the first person someone finds out about online lessons from and they like your site and YouTube videos, they may well not even bother searching for other possible teachers and just choose you.

There's little else you can learn about teaching without giving it a go, earning some money and gaining experience on the job. Be yourself, be flexible and never be afraid to throw the lesson plan in the bin! Have a great time passing your knowledge and craft on to others and helping your students to experience the enjoyment and fun of playing the drums.

Acknowledgements

I'd like to say a huge thank you to the following people without whom, for various reasons, this book wouldn't exist:

Vikki, Jack, Craig, Tim, Martin and David.

Special thanks to Sinne, Hannah, Mum and Dad for their continued encouragement and support, and for putting up with all the noise!

Printed in Great Britain
by Amazon.co.uk, Ltd.,
Marston Gate.